Build Your Vocabulary 3

John Flower

with

Michael Berman
and
Mark Powell

LTP
LANGUAGE

LANGUAGE TEACHING PUBLICATIONS
35 Church Road, Hove, BN3 2BE, England

ISBN 0 906717 78 7

New Edition 1994

The Author
John Flower is a teacher at Eurocentre Bournemouth where he has worked for many years. He has long experience of students at all levels and has prepared many students for the Cambridge examinations. He is the author of First Certificate Organiser, Phrasal Verb Organiser, and Build Your Business Vocabulary.

Personal Note
The author would like to express his thanks to Michael Lewis for his enthusiasm and guidance, to Michael Berman who contributed some lively ideas for alternative ways to build vocabulary, and to Mark Powell for some more lexical exercises for this new edition. He would also like to thank his colleagues and students for their help, his wife for typing and advice, and his children for not making too much noise!

Acknowledgements
Cover Design by Anna Macleod.
Illustrations by James Slater.
Ideas for illustrations from Argos.
Printed in England by Commercial Colour Press, London E7.

Contents

Read this before you start

So you plan to build your vocabulary! Learning vocabulary is a very important part of learning English. If you make a grammar mistake, it may be “wrong” but very often people will understand you anyway. But if you don’t know the exact word that you need, it is very frustrating for you, and the person you are talking to. Good English means having a big vocabulary!

There are better and worse ways to build your vocabulary and this book will help you to build your vocabulary quickly and effectively.
You will find it is best to work:

- systematically
- regularly
- personally

Don’t just make lists of all the new words you meet — plan and choose. Think of areas **you** are interested in; look for things **you** can’t say in English, then fill those gaps in **your** vocabulary.

Don’t do ten pages one day then nothing for three weeks! Try to do one or two pages every day. Regular work will help you to build effectively.

Don’t just learn words; you also need to know how to use them. Which words does a word often combine with? This book will help you to learn more words, but also how to use the words you know more effectively. That is an important part of building your vocabulary.

Don’t just use your dictionary when you have problems. It is an important resource. It can help you in lots of different ways. There are tips all through this book to help you use your dictionary effectively.

Don’t just make lists of new words; organise them. Again, there are tips to help you to learn and remember more of what you study.

Finally, there are a lot of words in English. Building your vocabulary is a long job! There are two more books in this series to help you learn more words, and to help you to enjoy the job!

1 Building your vocabulary

If you want to **build your vocabulary**, a good English-English dictionary is a necessary resource. Very often students only use their dictionaries when they need to find out what an individual word means. But a good dictionary should be much more useful than that! A dictionary will help you with pronunciation, meaning of individual words, useful idioms or other fixed expressions. Most usefully of all, it will tell you which words often combine with a particular word. The practices in this book will help you; they will help you a lot more if you use them beside a good English-English dictionary.

A. Pronunciation

Which word on the right rhymes with the word on the left? You may need your dictionary!

1. **aisle**	I'll	ail	ill
2. **own**	drown	crown	grown
3. **word**	sword	ward	bird
4. **deign**	plain	scene	decline

You don't know a word until you are sure how to pronounce it. Always check when you meet a new word.

B. Meaning

Often students ask *'What does this word mean?'* but it isn't always so easy to say. It depends on the context — the other words near the word. Lots of words have more than one meaning; sometimes similar meanings, sometimes quite different. You can **build your vocabulary** by learning new meanings for words you already know.

How many meanings can you think of for each of these words? When you have answered, check with your English-English dictionary.

	Meanings I know	**Number of meanings in dictionary**
1. **grave**	....	....
2. **light**	....	....
3. **drive**	....	....
4. **see**	....	....

Using your dictionary can help you to understand **extra** uses of words you already know and, perhaps, the limits of when you **cannot** use a word. Let your dictionary help you!

C. Word formation

Very often you learn a word but not the other members of its family. Many words have a family of associated words — noun, adjective, verb, adverb. If there are one or two members of the family which you do not know you may have to twist your grammar to avoid the word you don't know. A very efficient way to **build your vocabulary** is to make sure you know the different grammatical forms of the same basic word, for example:

bright	**brighten**	**brightness**	**brightly**
doubt (n)	**doubt (v)**	**doubtful**	**doubtfully**
vary	**variation**	**variable**	**variability**

Use the correct form of the word given in brackets to complete the sentence.

1. I'm losing . . . . Nothing seems to be happening! (PATIENT)
2. This skirt is too short. It needs . . . . (LENGTH)
3. What sort of . . . . will there be at the party? (ENTERTAIN)
4. He's a very good . . . . (MUSIC)

D. Word partnerships

One of the most important things you need to know to **build your vocabulary** successfully is to learn how words join together. Some phrases are fixed in the language, and you need to learn these.

Do you use the verb **do** or the verb **make** with these? You may need to check in your dictionary again.

1. . . . . some cleaning
2. . . . . a silly mistake
3. . . . . the right thing
4. . . . . a good impression
5. . . . . somebody a good turn
6. . . . . the wrong decision

Sometimes the phrases are not fixed, but they are 'nearly fixed', the words very often occur together. Again, you need to learn words with their partners to make your English fluent and natural.

Can you make five natural pairs which often occur together from these groups?

foreseeable	change	. . . .
golden	excuse	. . . .
lame	past	. . . .
radical	opportunity	. . . .
recent	future	. . . .

The practices in this book help you to **build your vocabulary** in different ways. They will help you to speak more natural, and more fluent English.

2 Expressions with 'what'

Complete the following expressions using the adjective which fits best with the meaning of each sentence.

interested depressed irritated shocked

1. What . . . . me was the way he expected ME to pay the bill!
2. What . . . . me was the huge number of beggars in the streets.
3. What . . . . me was the way he drank whisky at breakfast.
4. What . . . . me was the strange history of the place.

surprised annoyed pleased upset

5. What . . . . me was how hard-working Jane proved to be.
6. What . . . . me was the fact that she forgot my birthday again.
7. What . . . . me was that it was half an hour before the waiter arrived.
8. What . . . . me was that the food in Britain turned out to be so good.

disappointed fascinated amazed amused

9. What . . . . me was that she remembered me after 50 years.
10. What . . . . us was that the beach was not as clean as in the brochure.
11. What . . . . us was when he lost his contact lens in her soup!
12. What . . . . me was the incredible skill of the local craftsmen.

HOLIDAY MEMORIES

annoying disappointing shocking interesting amusing amazing

13. What was absolutely . . . . was the spectacular scenery just outside town.
14. What was particularly . . . . was listening to the British tourists trying to speak the language.
15. What was most . . . . was the tour of the ancient Roman ruins.
16. What was especially . . . . was that it rained for 5 of the 7 days.
17. What was so . . . . was the terrible noise coming from the discos all night.
18. What was really . . . . was the filthy beach.

3 Word partnerships – 1

Remember that learning word partnerships may be a better way to build your vocabulary than just learning miscellaneous new words.

Match each adjective on the left with a noun on the right. Use each word once only. Write your answers in the boxes.

Set 1

1. compulsive	a. answers
2. constructive	b. behaviour
3. evasive	c. criticism
4. exhaustive	d. gambler
5. expensive	e. heat
6. impressive	f. plot
7. impulsive	g. results
8. inventive	h. society
9. oppressive	i. tastes
10. permissive	j. tests

1	
2	
3	
4	
5	
6	
7	
8	
9	
10	

Set 2

Now do the same with these words.

1. confidential	a. buy
2. critical	b. experience
3. economical	c. illness
4. fanatical	d. information
5. hysterical	e. moment
6. magical	f. reaction
7. mystical	g. relationships
8. personal	h. review
9. psychological	i. supporters
10. terminal	j. tests

1	
2	
3	
4	
5	
6	
7	
8	
9	
10	

You may find more than one noun will fit with some of the adjectives. Try to find a complete set of common natural expressions. One suggested set is given in the answers.

4 Word formation — 1

As you read and listen to English, notice examples of word formation. Some nouns for example, can be formed by adding **-al**,**-ment** or **-tion** to a verb. Sometimes changes in spelling are necessary, for example:

try	trial
argue	argument
inform	information

Because word formation rules are very general, people sometimes invent words, which it is immediately possible to understand. Don't be afraid to try this yourself! Can you understand these words:

copiability
openness

Are they in your English Dictionary?

Complete each sentence by forming a noun from the verb in brackets.

1. He made an . . . . for the position of manager. (APPLY)

2. We need her . . . . before we can go ahead. (APPROVE)

3. He made an . . . . to see me at two o'clock. (ARRANGE)

4. Have you got . . . . of your booking yet? (CONFIRM)

5. This time his . . . . were not believed. (DENY)

6. This new centre is an interesting . . . . (DEVELOP)

7. He sued the company for unfair . . . . (DISMISS)

8. I'm afraid . . . . is hard to find round here. (EMPLOY)

9. She made a thorough . . . . of the body. (EXAMINE)

10. He gave no . . . . for his absence. (EXPLAIN)

11. I hope to be a minister in the next . . . . (GOVERN)

12. Has she got any kind of . . . . on her? (IDENTIFY)

13. His . . . . definitely needs working on. (PRONOUNCE)

14. He made a . . . . to proceed with the sale. (RECOMMEND)

15. We were shocked by his . . . . to see his son. (REFUSE)

16. I wish you a very happy . . . . (RETIRE)

5 Phrasal verbs — 1

Use the words on the left to make two-word verbs. Complete the table on the right to show the meaning of each verb.

1 TURN		2 DO		3 TAKE
	4 CALL		5 CUT	
6 WORK		7 LOOK		8 HOLD
	9 PUT		10 GET	
A FOR		B AFTER		C OFF
	D DOWN		E OUT	
F UP		G FORWARD		H ON
	I AT		J IN	

CALCULATE	6	
COLLECT		A
DECORATE	2	
GO TO BED		J
PROTECT	7	
REACH		I
REDUCE	5	
REMOVE		C
SUGGEST	9	
WAIT		H

Use the phrasal verbs to complete each of these sentences:

1. What time did you . . . . last night?
2. Will you be ready if I . . . . you at half past eight?
3. You've got nothing to worry about because I promise I'll . . . . you.
4. I had to . . . . my clothes so that the doctor could examine me.
5. Place the medicine on the top shelf of the bathroom cabinet so that the children can't . . . . it.
6. When I've got the money, I'd like to have the bathroom . . . .
7. When you've . . . . the total, don't forget to add VAT.
8. If you find my idea unacceptable, why don't you . . . . an alternative?
9. I'll be patient for as long as I can but I can't . . . . for ever.
10. You should try to . . . . the number of cigarettes you smoke.

6 Relationships

Choose the word or phrase which best completes each sentence. Give one answer only to each question:

1. For years I've .... of meeting someone like you!
a. hoped **b.** wished **c.** longed **d.** dreamed

2. I'd ask you to marry me but I'm sure you'd turn me ....
a. around **b.** down **c.** off **d.** over

3. Sometimes we have to .... our feelings.
a. compress **b.** depress **c.** oppress **d.** repress

4. A good friend will always .... you when you're in trouble.
a. stand by **b.** stand up **c.** stand for **d.** stand up against

5. Unfortunately their marriage is ....
a. on the rocks **b.** out of order **c.** out of sorts **d.** on the decline

6. I'm absolutely .... about her but she doesn't seem very interested in me.
a. overwhelmed **b.** crazy **c.** infatuated **d.** sick

7. They don't get on well with each other because they're ....
a. disaffected **b.** dissident **c.** incompatible **d.** incongruous

8. The moment I saw you it was love ....
a. at a glance **b.** into view **c.** at first sight **d.** out of focus

9. I've got no .... of getting married. I'm a confirmed bachelor.
a. aim **b.** intention **c.** plan **d.** desire

10. It's .... knowledge that they're going out with each other.
a. common **b.** frequent **c.** general **d.** open

11. It's said that absence makes the heart grow ....
a. fonder **b.** loving **c.** stronger **d.** affectionate

12. Instead of feeling sorry for yourself, it's time you got to .... with your problem.
a. fare **b.** tackle **c.** grips **d.** wrestle

13. You've got no right to blame me for everything — it takes two to .... a quarrel.
a. do **b.** look for **c.** make **d.** want

14. It's a great shame that you .... with each other as you used to be such good friends.
a. came out **b.** fell out **c.** set out **d.** turned out

15. It's time we had a .... talk with each other in an effort to clear the air.
a. eye-to-eye **b.** heart-to-heart **c.** face-to-face **d.** cheek-to-cheek

16. Since we got divorced, we've gone our own separate ....
a. directions **b.** lives **c.** paths **d.** ways

17. He .... into her eyes and declared his love for her.
a. glanced **b.** glared **c.** gazed **d.** glimpsed

18. Although they no longer love each other, they've decided to stay together .... the children.
a. for the sake of **b.** in spite of **c.** on behalf of **d.** in the event of

7 Using a trade directory

In a trade directory services and suppliers are listed under appropriate headings.
In this exercise you have to decide which heading from the following list you would look under for what you need. Use each heading once only.
Write your answers in the boxes.

1. **BLACKSMITHS**
2. **BUILDERS**
3. **DENTAL SURGEONS**
4. **ENTERTAINERS**
5. **ESTATE AGENTS**
6. **GENEALOGISTS**
7. **HYPNOTHERAPISTS**
8. **LEGAL SERVICES**
9. **OFFICE SUPPLIES**
10. **PEST CONTROL**
11. **PLACES OF WORSHIP**
12. **PLUMBERS**
13. **SECURITY EQUIPMENT**
14. **TOOL REPAIRS**
15. **WASTE DISPOSAL**

PROBLEM

a. One of your pipes is leaking.
b. You want to sell your house.
c. You are frightened of being burgled.
d. There are rats in your house!
e. You want a magician for a party.
f. You have some rubbish you want taken away.
g. You want to buy a dictating machine.
h. Your roof has collapsed.
i. Someone has threatened to take you to court.
j. You want to trace your ancestors.
k. Your lawn mower has broken.
l. You want to go to church.
m. Your horse needs new shoes.
n. You're trying to give up smoking.
o. A filling has come out of one of your teeth.

1	
2	
3	
4	
5	
6	
7	
8	
9	
10	
11	
12	
13	
14	
15	

8 Homophones

You don't really know a word until you know how to pronounce it properly. This is why it is a good idea to learn the system of phonetic symbols used by your dictionary. This means that every time you look up the meaning of a word you can check its pronunciation.

Find which of the three words on the right is pronounced the same as the word on the left.

1.	bear	beer	bare	buyer
2.	caught	cord	court	coat
3.	fair	fare	fear	fire
4.	flour	flower	flare	floor
5.	groan	groin	grown	growing
6.	heel	hill	hail	heal
7.	hire	higher	high	hair
8.	mist	mess	mast	missed
9.	one	when	won	own
10.	pail	pale	pile	peel
11.	peace	pies	peas	piece
12.	pear	peer	pier	pair
13.	road	wrote	rude	rode
14.	sail	seal	sell	sale
15.	sent	scent	send	saint
16.	sweet	sweat	suite	suit
17.	weak	wake	week	wick
18.	whole	whale	hole	wall

9 Guess the subject

In most countries, it is possible to receive radio programmes in English. Listening to the news and other programmes will help you improve your English.

If you don't hear or don't understand everything, don't worry. It is often possible to guess what people are talking about because you hear other words that go very closely with a subject. For example, if you hear the words:

headlights, hatchback, accelerate, overtake

the people are probably talking about motoring.

What is 'it' in each of these sentences? Write your answer in the space provided.

1. If it's that sore, I would gargle with salt water and speak as little as possible. ....

2. She baked it specially for his birthday. ....

3. After washing it, she put some curlers in as she wanted it to look good for the dance. ....

4. I had to apply another coat of it as I could still see the old one underneath. ....

5. They say it's so creamy because the cows are so contented! ....

6. Switch it on if you think it's too dark in here. ....

7. After they had inflated it, it flew up into some trees where unfortunately it burst. ....

8. It can be used transitively or intransitively. ....

9. It gets wider as it flows down to the sea. ....

10. It leaked and left an ink stain on my shirt. ....

11. When the doctor felt it, he found it was very irregular. ....

12. Don't squeeze it! The gun might go off! ....

13. Unfortunately it's flat so we'll have to get the spare from the boot. ....

14. It kept me awake with all its barking. ....

10 What's missing?

Under each picture write the name of the item and what is missing. Choose from the following list of words.

beard	**man**	**spoke**
flower	**petal**	**stem**
glass	**plug**	**strap**
hairdryer	**rung**	**suitcase**
lace	**shoe**	**taps**
ladder	**sink**	**wheel**

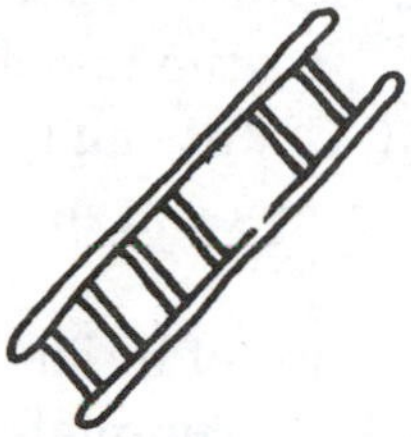

1. ....
....

2. ....
....

3. ....
....

4. ....
....

5. ....
....

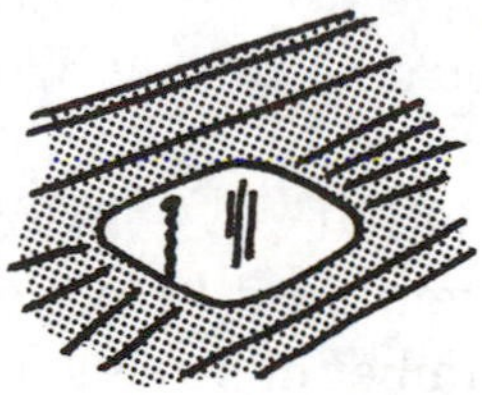

6. ....
....

7. ....
....

8. ....
....

9. ....
....

11 A bite to eat

Choose the word or phrase which best completes each sentence. Give one answer only to each question:

1. Indian food's too spicy for my . . . .
   a. appetite **b.** desire **c.** flavour **d.** liking
2. You do the cooking and I'll wash up . . . .
   a. in return **b.** by return **c.** in revenge **d.** to reciprocate
3. Air, food and water are . . . . to life.
   a. indispensable **b.** inevitable **c.** indisputable **d.** indestructible
4. The inconvenience of going on a diet is . . . . by the benefits.
   a. overbalanced **b.** outranked **c.** overthrown **d.** outweighed
5. The kitchen has been designed so that all the things you need are conveniently . . . .
   a. to hand **b.** in hand **c.** by hand **d.** out of hand
6. Dieticians have recently . . . . suggestions for a complete reform in our eating habits.
   a. come up to **b.** put forward **c.** made up **d.** taken out
7. Teetotallers . . . . from drinking alcohol.
   a. avert **b.** abstain **c.** evade **d.** abscond
8. You'd better not drink too much of that stuff. It's extremely . . . .
   a. lethal **b.** toxic **c.** potent **d.** fatal
9. If you want to lose weight, you should . . . . the number of sweets and chocolates you eat.
   a. come down with **b.** take out of **c.** cut down on **d.** watch out for
10. Chocolate cake's an irresistible temptation for somebody who's got a sweet . . . .
    a. appetite **b.** palate **c.** taste **d.** tooth
11. If there's no coffee left, we'll have to . . . . tea.
    a. do up with **b.** make do with **c.** do away with **d.** make up with
12. The tomatoes are still green — they aren't . . . . yet.
    a. developed **b.** mature **c.** ripe **d.** seasoned
13. If there's one thing I can't . . . . it's soggy vegetables.
    a. appeal to **b.** bare **c.** support **d.** bear
14. The pudding was so delicious I had a second . . . .
    a. go **b.** helping **c.** plate **d.** serving

12 Word partnerships – 2

Match each word on the left with a noun on the right. Use each word once only. Write your answers in the boxes.

You may find more than one set of possibilities. Try to choose only common natural expressions; word partnerships which **often** occur together.

Set 1

1.	accurate	**a.**	addiction
2.	artificial	**b.**	communication
3.	comprehensive	**c.**	condition
4.	drug	**d.**	destination
5.	final	**e.**	education
6.	irresistible	**f.**	organisation
7.	perfect	**g.**	prediction
8.	substantial	**h.**	reduction
9.	underground	**i.**	respiration
10.	verbal	**j.**	temptation

1	
2	
3	
4	
5	
6	
7	
8	
9	
10	

Set 2

Now do the same with these words.

1.	difficult	**a.**	admission
2.	foregone	**b.**	conclusion
3.	free	**c.**	confusion
4.	gentle	**d.**	conversion
5.	official	**e.**	decision
6.	optical	**f.**	diversion
7.	religious	**g.**	evasion
8.	tax	**h.**	illusion
9.	total	**i.**	permission
10.	traffic	**j.**	persuasion

1	
2	
3	
4	
5	
6	
7	
8	
9	
10	

13 Expressions with 'on'

Remember to keep looking for examples of words which combine together to form common expressions.

There are several expressions in English using prepositions. If you look up one of these expressions in a dictionary you will sometimes find it under the preposition. Sometimes, however, you have to look under the noun. Remember, learning word combinations is an important way to build your vocabulary.

Here are some expressions with '**on**'. Make sure you understand them before doing the exercise.

on approval	**on behalf of**	**on condition that**
on the contrary	**on credit**	**on a diet**
on display	**on fire**	**on foot**
on holiday	**on purpose**	**on strike**
on trial	**on the way**	

Put the correct word(s) from the above list into the following sentences. Use each expression once only.

1. He's so calm! You wouldn't think he was on . . . . for murder, would you?
2. I'm on . . . . I simply must lose some weight!
3. The building must be on . . . . Why else would the alarm be ringing?
4. I bumped into her on . . . . to work this morning.
5. That was no accident! You did it on . . . . !
6. She saw the dress on . . . . in the shop window.
7. She's away on . . . . in Spain this week.
8. They've let us have this word processor on . . . . so that we can try one out before we decide.
9. They let him stay on . . . . he worked harder.
10. I got this car on . . . . and there are still another ten payments to go.
11. We came to work on . . . . today as part of our fitness campaign.
12. I am writing to you on . . . . Miss Jones, who unfortunately has had to go into hospital.
13. The drivers went on . . . . for better conditions.
14. I don't hate him. On . . . . , I like him very much.

14 Confusing words — 1

If you have difficulty remembering how a word is used, write a sentence with the word in it. A good dictionary will show you the word in a phrase or sentence and you should look out for other examples while you are reading or listening to English.

You are more likely to remember the word if you write an amusing, personal or otherwise memorable sentence.

Choose the correct word for each sentence.

1. The *audience / spectators* cheered when he scored the goal.
2. What happened had no *affect / effect* on the result.
3. They live in a beautiful house *beside / besides* the sea.
4. I want to introduce the subject *briefly / shortly* now, and then discuss it in detail next week.
5. I must know your answer *by / until* 5 o'clock.
6. I did very little work because of the *continual / continuous* interruptions.
7. They *controlled / inspected* the luggage with their X-ray equipment to see if there was a bomb inside.
8. We haven't seen him *during / for* 6 years.
9. The newspaper *headline / title* said 'Famous Writer Killed'
10. His writing is so *imaginary / imaginative*. I especially like his description of the storm.
11. You need a work *permission / permit* to get a job here.
12. I expect taxes to *raise / rise* in the next few weeks.
13. They will change goods if you have a *receipt / recipe*.
14. Could you *sew / sow* on this button for me?
15. There's such beautiful *scene / scenery* around here.
16. You could see the man's *shade / shadow* on the wall.
17. Get some paper from the *stationary / stationery* cupboard.
18. They *wandered / wondered* around, looking at the shops.

Now see if you can make your own sentences using any words you had difficulty with.

15 Formal English

When you learn English, it is important to know the appropriate situation or context for the words you use. In some dictionaries you will see the abbreviation **fml** to indicate that a word is an example of formal English. This kind of word is mainly used in the written form of the language, for example in business letters and reports.

A. Complete each sentence by using the correct word from the following list. Use each word once only. At the end of each sentence write a simple conversational word or expression that means the same as the word you have used.

advise	**comprehend**	**require**
cease	**exceed**	**respond**
commence	**purchase**	**seek**

1. The meeting did not . . . . on time as some participants were delayed. (. . . . .)

2. I fail to . . . . how such a mistake could have been made. (. . . . .)

3. We hope to . . . . to your letter as soon as possible. (. . . . .)

4. We shall . . . . you when the goods have arrived. (. . . . .)

5. She did not have enough money to . . . . the necessary equipment. (. . . . .)

6. This car will . . . . a service every six months. (. . . . .)

7. Our profits should . . . . ten million pounds this year. (. . . . .)

8. Hostilities will . . . . at midnight and we shall have peace at last. (. . . . .)

9. We had to . . . . the answer elsewhere. (. . . . .)

I apologise for causing you any inconvenience but I am endeavouring to ascertain the whereabouts of the station.

B. Now do the same with these sentences. Choose from the following words:

adhere	**decline**	**remit**
ascertain	**encounter**	**remunerate**
augment	**obtain**	**terminate**

1. He unfortunately has to . . . . your kind invitation. (. . . . .)

2. They decided to . . . . to their original plan despite the added complications. (. . . . .)

3. Near the end of the film they . . . . a strange old man living in a cave. (. . . . .)

4. Please . . . . your payment to the above address. (. . . . .)

5. We have decided to . . . . our agreement because of the problems that have arisen. (. . . . .)

6. She was unable to . . . . what exactly had happened. (. . . . . . .)

7. We shall of course . . . . employees in the normal way for working these extra hours.(. . . . .)

8. He failed to . . . . the necessary permit to work in the country. (. . . . .)

9. She had to . . . . her income by working in the evenings. (. . . . .)

16 Hobbies

Use what you see and do in your everyday life to build your vocabulary. Have you got any hobbies? Write a list of all the English words you know which can be associated with these activities. If there are any words you don't know, try to find the words and how to say them.

Complete the diagram below by choosing items from the following list. Each item is usually associated with one of the four hobbies. Use each item once only. The first item has been done for you as an example.

buttons	**fork**	**needles**	**spade**
camera	**hammer**	**pattern**	**tape measure**
chisel	**hoe**	**pins**	**thimble**
film	**hose**	**plane**	**thread**
filters	**lens**	**rake**	**tripod**
flash	**light meter**	**saw**	**trowel**
flowerpots	**nails**	**screws**	**vice**

Dressmaking

Gardening

Photography

Woodwork

17 Health

Choose the word or phrase which best completes each sentence. Give one answer only to each question:

1. Unless you give up smoking, you . . . . the risk of damaging your health.
   a. bear **b.** suffer **c.** make **d.** run

2. I'm feeling . . . . and could do with a holiday.
   a. run across **b.** run down **c.** run out **d.** run over

3. The drugs the doctor prescribed made me feel . . . .
   a. drowsy **b.** wary **c.** dreary **d.** dowdy

4. Being a nurse sometimes . . . . looking after difficult patients.
   a. curtails **b.** details **c.** entails **d.** retails

5. The . . . . you gain from physical exercise are well worth the effort.
   a. profits **b.** benefits **c.** advantages **d.** improvements

6. The patient's health has . . . . so much that the doctors fear for his life.
   a. declined **b.** degenerated **c.** disintegrated **d.** deteriorated

7. The idea of a balanced diet is difficult to . . . . to those who know little about food values.
   a. come across **b.** take in **c.** make over **d.** put across

8. You should take an aspirin or something to help . . . . the pain.
   a. lighten **b.** calm **c.** relieve **d.** rid

9. If you've got a sore throat, you should . . . . with salt water.
a. gargle **b.** giggle **c.** gurgle **d.** guzzle

10. . . . . you're a millionaire, you can't buy health and happiness.
a. Besides **b.** Except that **c.** Even if **d.** Despite

11. You don't look well — You're a bit . . . .
a. off colour **b.** off health **c.** off vigour **d.** off fitness

12. . . . . the patient's condition, the doctor decided to operate.
a. According to **b.** In the event of **c.** In view of **d.** Regarding

13. Now that the patient's . . . . , she should be out of hospital in no time at all.
a. on the recovery **b.** on the mend
c. on the improvement **d.** on the repair

14. I've got a . . . . headache and all I feel like doing is going straight to bed.
a. beating **b.** drumming **c.** hammering **d.** splitting

15. The new discovery was an important . . . . in the fight against cancer.
a. daybreak **b.** break-away **c.** outbreak **d.** breakthrough

16. The . . . . against the baby being deformed are about 1,000 to 1.
a. possibilities **b.** figures **c.** opportunities **d.** odds

17. Now that I've discovered that I'm . . . . strawberries, I make sure I never eat them.
a. allergic against **b.** allergic from **c.** allergic to **d.** allergic with

18. You're to take a . . . . of this medicine three times a day.
a. ration **b.** helping **c.** dose **d.** portion

18 Expressions with 'make'

Don't forget to keep looking out for common word partnerships as you listen to and read English.

You will find that there are several expressions containing the verb '**make**'. If you need to look up the meaning, you may find them under 'make' or under the other part of the expression.

Complete the sentences by using the following words.
Use each word once only.

amends	**day**	**fortune**	**point**
attempt	**difference**	**fun**	**sense**
bed	**ends**	**offer**	**statement**
contact	**example**	**pass**	**way**

1. It makes no . . . . to me how old he is
2. He bought her flowers to make . . . . for being late.
3. When he made a . . . . at her, she slapped his face.
4. Since he made a . . . . in property development, he's been living a life of luxury.
5. Somebody's made an . . . . on the President's life!
6. She made him an . . . . of £3 million for his business.
7. It really made her . . . . to see you all again.
8. The judge decided to make an . . . . of him and sentenced him to ten years' imprisonment.
9. The only way you can make . . . . with them is by radio.
10. They made . . . . of the awkward way he walked.
11. On her salary she had difficulty making . . . . meet.
12. The minister made a . . . . about the new proposal.
13. Remember to use clean sheets when you make the . . . .
14. The boss made a . . . . of meeting every employee.
15. They made their . . . . to the stadium on foot.
16. Help! I can't make . . . . of this exercise!

Now underline all the work partnerships which include part of the verb '**make**'.

19 Stress patterns

> If you stress a word wrongly, it makes you very difficult to understand. Stress is often more important than perfect pronunciation. This is why it is important to check the stress of every word you learn.

In this exercise you must put each of the words below into the correct list depending on its stress pattern.
The sign ▼ shows the main stress.
The first word is shown as an example.

accommodation	**decorator**	**electricity**	**investigation**
apologetic	**decorations**	**electronic**	**opportunity**
approximately	**dedicated**	**entertainment**	**refrigerator**
certificate	**dedication**	**enthusiastic**	**representative**
competitively	**delivery**	**impossible**	**speculator**
competitor	**deteriorate**	**international**	**tranquilliser**

1. ▼○○○

. . . .

. . . .

. . . .

. . . .

2. ○▼○○

. . . .

. . . .

. . . .

. . . .

3. ○○▼○

. . . .

. . . .

. . . .

. . . .

4. ○▼○○○

. . . .

. . . .

. . . .

. . . .

5. ○○▼○○

. . . .

. . . .

. . . .

. . . .

6. ○○○▼○

accommodation

. . . .

. . . .

. . . .

20 Body idioms — 1

There are a number of expressions in English containing words referring to parts of the body.

It is important to remember, however, that if you have similar types of expressions in your language, they might not translate word for word into English. If you attempt to translate idioms literally into another language, people often have no idea what you are talking about!

Complete each sentence with the correct part of the body.
Choose from the following words. Some are used more than once.

back	**ear**	**hair**	**leg**
blood	**eye**	**hand**	**mouth**
bone	**face**	**heart**	**teeth**
breast	**foot**	**head**	**tooth**

1. You have a free . . . . You can work with whoever you like.

2. The way he plays the violin sets my . . . . on edge.

3. The sight of those ghostly figures made his . . . . run cold.

4. I have a . . . . to pick with you! Where's that book you promised?

5. She has a very cool . . . . so she didn't panic.

6. He made a clean . . . . of it and admitted he was the one who had stolen the money.

7. The way they treated the animals made my . . . . boil.

8. The soldiers were armed to the . . . .

9. She got a pat on the . . . . for doing such a good job.

10. He turned a deaf . . . . to my request for more money.

11. They always criticise her behind her . . . .

12. I can't understand this. It's way above my . . . .

13. I want you to learn these words by . . . . before the next lesson.

14. That's just what I was going to say! You took the words right out of my . . . .

15. Relax! Let your . . . . down for a change!

16. Could you give me a . . . . with this ladder?

17. I'll keep an . . . . on your cat while you're away.

18. That can't be true! You're pulling my . . . . !

19. You've really put your . . . . in it this time! Whatever made you say such a thing?

20. We were all shocked but she didn't turn a . . . .

21. He was too frightened to say it to her . . . .

22. We could wait for the next bus. On the other . . . . , we could walk.

23. She pulled a long . . . . when we told her our plans.

24. You know what a sweet . . . . he's got so don't leave that box of chocolates lying around.

21 Science and technology

Choose the best alternative to complete each sentence.
Look up any words you don't know.

1. My microscope can . . . . objects up to a hundred times.
a. amplify **b.** extend **c.** generate **d.** magnify

2. The sponge . . . . most of the water.
a. ate **b.** absorbed **c.** digested **d.** exhausted

3. The . . . . on the window shows that it's cold outside.
a. condensation **b.** damp **c.** evaporation **d.** humidity

4. The water . . . . out of the hole in the dam.
a. flowed **b.** floated **c.** expanded **d.** drifted

5. From this terminal you can call . . . . our main computer at head office.
a. on **b.** for **c.** at **d.** up

6. Robot arms . . . . the parts of the car together.
a. melt **b.** weld **c.** sew **d.** saw

7. Electronically stored information is easily . . . .
a. resumed **b.** updated **c.** predated **d.** rebuilt

8. They heard the aeroplane go through the sound . . . .
a. barrier **b.** limit **c.** junction **d.** frontier

9. The drill . . . . a hole 20 metres deep.
a. poured **b.** pierced **c.** bored **d.** fixed

10. Tall buildings must have strong . . . . to stand on.
a. funds **b.** fundamentals **c.** foundations **d.** basics

11. I picked . . . . radio signals from all over the world.
a. on **b.** at **c.** up **d.** off

12. A long . . . . was dug to put the pipes in.
a. canal **b.** pile **c.** path **d.** trench

13. Nowadays international telephone calls are beamed into space and . . . . off satellites.
a. bumped **b.** bounced **c.** jumped **d.** radiated

14. Thousands of circuits can be . . . . onto one microchip.
a. crammed **b.** crushed **c.** cranked **d.** crunched

15. I couldn't receive the programme very clearly because of . . . . caused by the weather conditions.
a. blocks **b.** blockage **c.** interference **d.** manipulation

22 Word partnerships – 3

Match the verb on the left with a noun on the right. Use each word once only. Write your answers in the boxes.

Set 1

1.	agonise	a.	a building
2.	apologise	b.	over decisions
3.	hospitalise	c.	facts and figures
4.	memorise	d.	innocent victims
5.	modernise	e.	your life
6.	organise	f.	your limitations
7.	realise	g.	for your mistakes
8.	specialise	h.	a patient
9.	terrorise	i.	a phone box
10.	vandalise	j.	in tropical medicine

1	
2	
3	
4	
5	
6	
7	
8	
9	
10	

Set 2

Now do the same with these words.

1.	alleviate	a.	an agreement
2.	captivate	b.	the audience
3.	cultivate	c.	a celebrity
4.	eradicate	d.	a crime
5.	generate	e.	a criminal
6.	impersonate	f.	electricity
7.	interrogate	g.	your garden
8.	investigate	h.	in oil shares
9.	speculate	i.	the pain
10.	terminate	j.	a problem

1	
2	
3	
4	
5	
6	
7	
8	
9	
10	

Remember learning words in partnerships will help you to make your English more natural and more effective.

23 Everyday conversations

Complete each of these conversations with an appropriate response. Use each response once only. Write the response under the picture. Choose from these responses:

Responses

a. Neither can I.
b. Let's hope so!
c. You're telling me!
d. What's the point?
e. Serves you right.
f. That could be tricky!
g. How embarrassing!
h. You might as well.
i. I don't blame you!
j. About time too!

1. ....

2. ....

3. ....

4. ....

I HAD £10 DEDUCTED FROM MY WAGES FOR TURNING UP LATE.

5. ....

THEN SUDDENLY MY BELT BROKE AND MY TROUSERS FELL DOWN.

6. ....

THE MUSIC IS DEAFENING, ISN'T IT ?

7. ....

DO YOU THINK THIS RAIN WILL STOP SOON ?

8. ....

SHALL I SHUT UP SHOP NOW ?

9. ....

I CAN'T STAND SPICY FOOD.

10. ....

24 Opposites — verbs

Build your vocabulary by asking yourself if you know the opposite of one of the most important words in a sentence.

Notice how the opposite of a word often depends on its context. This is why it is important to learn words in a sentence, not in isolation.

Complete each sentence with the opposite of the word in brackets. Choose from one of the following words. Use each word once only and make sure you use the correct form.

abandon	**deteriorate**	**lower**	**reward**
defend	**fall**	**refuse**	**set**
demolish	**forbid**	**reject**	**simplify**
deny	**loosen**	**retreat**	**withdraw**

1. I was sure they would . . . . his proposal. (ACCEPT)

2. She . . . . that she had stolen the money. (ADMIT)

3. When the bugle sounded, the enemy . . . . (ADVANCE)

4. He . . . . to help the last time I asked him. (AGREE)

5. The crowd got excited as United desperately . . . . the goal. (ATTACK)

6. He's going to . . . . ten houses on the site. (BUILD)

7. These new regulations will of course. . . . . the situation. (COMPLICATE)

8. Will they . . . . the search if they haven't found her by this evening? (CONTINUE)

9. She's gone to the bank to . . . . some money. (DEPOSIT)

10. As time passed, his condition slowly . . . . (IMPROVE)

11. Smoking is . . . . in this part of the cinema. (PERMIT)

12. He expected to be . . . . for what he'd done. (PUNISH)

13. They've . . . . the ticket price to £3. (RAISE)

14. At what time will the sun . . . . tomorrow? (RISE)

15. The temperature should . . . . by five degrees. (RISE)

16. You need to . . . . the straps a little. (TIGHTEN)

25 Expressions with 'get'

Set 1

All the expressions on the left contain 'get'. Match them up with the equivalents on the right:

1. Get lost!
2. We're getting nowhere!
3. I don't get you.
4. OK, I get the message.
5. Now we're getting somewhere!
6. You're getting on my nerves.
7. Do you get me?
8. Let's get cracking.
9. I don't get it.
10. Get a move on!

a. I don't understand it.
b. I don't understand what you're saying.
c. Do you understand what I'm saying?
d. Hurry up!
e. Let's start.
f. We're not making any progress.
g. At last we're making some progress.
h. Don't be unpleasant! I understand!
i. Go away!
j. You're annoying me.

1	2	3	4	5	6	7	8	9	10

Set 2

Complete these conversations using the following once each:

on away together through up over out round

1. When are you going to wash the car?
   >Don't worry! I'll get . . . . to it later.
2. I feel terrible about letting them down.
   >Don't worry. They'll get . . . . it.
3. We must get . . . . for a meal sometime.
   >Yes. How about next Friday?
4. Why did you say you'd work this weekend?
   >Well I can't get . . . . of it now.
5. I really wish you'd just get . . . . with it.
   >OK. OK. It'll be ready soon.
6. Do you think I'd get the job if I lied about my age?
   >I don't think you'd get . . . . with it.
7. What have you been getting . . . . to?
   >Oh, nothing much. Just the usual. Work, a bit of gardening . . . .
8. I just don't seem to be getting . . . . to you, do I?
   >What do you mean?

26 Who's in charge?

Match the person with the people or thing they are in charge of. Use each word once only. Write your answers in the boxes.

Set 1

1. an admiral
2. a captain
3. a chairman/chairperson
4. a curator
5. an editor
6. a governor
7. a president
8. a principal
9. a sister
10. an umpire

a. a college
b. a fleet of ships
c. a hospital ward
d. a meeting
e. a museum
f. a newspaper
g. a prison
h. a republic
i. a ship
j. a tennis match

1	
2	
3	
4	
5	
6	
7	
8	
9	
10	

Set 2

Now do the same with these words.

1. a captain
2. a chief
3. a conductor
4. a director
5. a general
6. a headmaster/headmistress
7. a manager/manageress
8. a matron
9. a prime minister
10. a ringmaster

a. actors in a film
b. an army
c. circus performers
d. a football team
e. a government
f. hospital nurses
g. an orchestra
h. shop assistants
i. a teaching staff
j. a tribe

1	
2	
3	
4	
5	
6	
7	
8	
9	
10	

27 Word groups

Remember to keep making lists of words associated with subjects you are interested in. As you learn new words, you can add them to your lists.

Put each of the words below into the correct list.
Use each word once only.

box office	**food mixer**	**leaf**	**stalls**
casualty	**footlights**	**root**	**toe**
clinic	**fridge**	**sink**	**trunk**
collar	**heel**	**sleeve**	**twig**
cooker	**lace**	**sole**	**ward**
cuff	**lapel**	**stage**	**X-ray**

1. HOSPITAL

....
....
....
....

2. JACKET

....
....
....
....

3. KITCHEN

....
....
....
....

4. SHOE

....
....
....
....

5. THEATRE

....
....
....
....

6. TREE

....
....
....
....

28 Motoring

Choose the word or phrase which best completes each sentence. Give one answer only to each question:

1. I'm sorry I'm late. I was .... in the traffic.
   a. held back **b.** held down **c.** held over **d.** held up
2. The bonnet of the car was badly .... in the crash.
   a. creased **b.** dented **c.** crumpled **d.** bruised

3. You should always carry a(n) .... tyre in case of a puncture.
   a. additional **b.** extra **c.** spare **d.** supplementary
4. You're not allowed to .... on the brow of a hill.
   a. by pass **b.** overtake **c.** pass by **d.** take over
5. Traffic is being .... from the main road while it's under repair.
   a. averted **b.** converted **c.** diverted **d.** perverted
6. We had a flat tyre, which .... our departure.
   a. detained **b.** sent back **c.** delayed **d.** called off
7. The larger your car is, the fewer kilometres it will .... to the litre.
   a. do **b.** give **c.** get **d.** make
8. The van was so badly damaged that it was a complete ....
   a. breakdown **b.** break up **c.** write-off **d.** ruin
9. There's something wrong with the engine but I can't .... the exact problem.
   a. focus **b.** highlight **c.** pinpoint **d.** point at

10. Unless you . . . . you're in danger of having an accident.
a. decrease **b.** reduce **c.** slow down **d.** retard

11. Instead of talking to me while you're driving, you should . . . . on the road.
a. concentrate **b.** give attention
c. pay attention **d.** be absorbed

12. The driver . . . . to avoid the child who ran out into the road.
a. deviated **b.** skidded **c.** dodged **d.** swerved

13. If he hadn't managed to brake . . . . , he'd have certainly killed him.
a. by the time **b.** for the time being
c. in the nick of time **d.** on time

14. During the rush hour, traffic often comes to a . . . .
a. standpoint **b.** stoppage **c.** standstill **d.** stand

15. The cyclist was knocked down by a lorry and received . . . . injuries.
a. lethal **b.** fatal **c.** mortal **d.** deadly

16. We were . . . . a mile of our destination when we ran out of petrol.
a. hardly **b.** inside **c.** only **d.** within

17. The two lorries were involved in a . . . . collision.
a. headlong **b.** head-on **c.** headstrong **d.** headway

18. If you take the . . . . you'll be able to avoid the town centre.
a. by-pass **b.** lay-by **c.** lay-out **d.** outlet

29 Word ladder

Change the top word into the word at the bottom. Use the clues to help you. Each time you change one letter only in the previous word. Sometimes you might not know the word but you can guess what is possible and check with your dictionary.
Remember, guessing and using a good dictionary are two important ways to help you to improve your English.

		BLACK
2.	A . . . . of flats.	
3.	It tells the time.	
4.	I heard the . . . . of the key in the lock.	
5.	A . . . . salesman acts smoothly and efficiently.	
6.	Not tight.	
7.	A small rough house.	
8.	A sea creature with sharp teeth.	
9.	The opposite of **blunt**.	
10.	You'll have to . . . . as there aren't enough.	
11.	Look fixedly.	
12.	The . . . . tyre is in the boot of the car.	
13.	Leave enough . . . . to write your name.	
14.	Don't put too much . . . . in the curry!	
15.	A pointed piece of metal.	
16.	We decided to go out, in . . . . of the weather.	
17.	The most important bone in your back.	
18.	I wish the sun would	
19.	The noise made by a miserable dog.	
20.	Opposite of **black**.	**WHITE**

30 Newspaper vocabulary

Complete the sentences by using the following words.
Use each word once only.

caption	**editorial**	**obituary**
cartoon	**feature**	**preview**
circulation	**gossip column**	**review**
comic strip	**headline**	**supplement**
crossword	**horoscope**	**tabloid**

1. The . . . . at the top of the page said 'TALKS FAIL'

2. The newspaper has increased its . . . . by 5,000 copies a day.

3. He was unhappy at some of the comments in the . . . . of his latest film.

4. I always turn to the . . . . first. I love reading about the private lives of famous people.

5. I like the . . . . they've put below this picture.

6. I prefer a . . . . newspaper because it's a more convenient size.

7. They did a full-page special . . . . on poverty in inner city areas.

8. She drew the political . . . . on the front page.

9. I must read my . . . . to see if I'm going to have a good day.

10. The critics went to a special . . . . of the musical, which opens next week.

11. In his . . . . it said he died of a heart attack.

12. The guide to the air show came as a free . . . . to the local newspaper.

13. I only need one more word to complete the . . . .

14. If there's an exciting . . . . , people will keep buying the newspaper to see what happens next.

15. There was a short but effective . . . . giving the newspaper's opinion of the new defence policy.

31 Animal idioms

Use one of the following words to complete each sentence.
Some words are used more than once.

bat	**bull**	**crow**	**pig**
bee	**cat**	**dog**	**rat**
bird	**chicken**	**horse**	**worm**

1. He managed to . . . . his way into her confidence.
2. I'm as blind as a . . . . without my glasses.
3. She's really got a . . . . in her bonnet about this new scheme.
4. He decided to take the . . . . by the horns and see the boss about his problem.

5. Don't let the . . . . out of the bag. This is supposed to be a secret.
6. No wonder he feels sick! He really made a . . . . of himself last night!
7. She may . . . . out when she realises what exactly she's let herself in for.
8. He's such an early . . . . that he usually arrives before anybody else.
9. I smelt a . . . . when he couldn't produce any means of identification.
10. It's about ten miles in that direction as the . . . . flies.
11. A thousand pounds! That's . . . . feed! We need at least a million!
12. Mary could win the competition, you know. She's a real dark . . . .
13. He won't change. You can't teach an old . . . . new tricks.
14. That speech of hers certainly set the . . . . among the pigeons.
15. Be careful! You're rushing around like a . . . . in a china shop!

Many of the expressions in this page are idioms. They are useful to understand, but they are difficult to use **exactly** the right way. Be careful if you decide to use them yourself!

32 Memory game

Can you name all the things in the picture?
Use each of these words once only:

ankle	**fence**	**mug**	**rug**
butterfly	**ghost**	**onion**	**safety pin**
cheque	**hair grip**	**pencil**	**shower**
doll	**hook**	**plaster**	**spider**
drinking straw	**iron**	**rake**	**wrist**

1. . . . .

2. . . . .

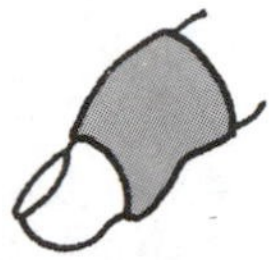
3. . . . .

4. . . . .

5. . . . .

6. . . . .

7. . . . .

8. . . . .

9. . . . .

10. . . . .

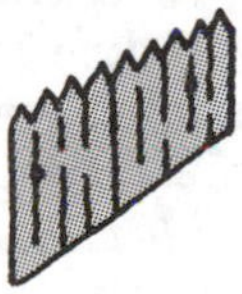
11. . . . .

12. . . . .

13. . . . .

14. . . . .

15. . . . .

16. . . . .

17. . . . .

18. . . . .

19. . . . .

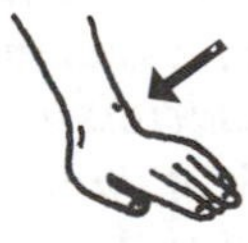
20. . . . .

Now look at the picture for one minute and then cover it. See how many of the objects you can remember.

33 Confusing words — 2

Some dictionaries give examples of English words which are commonly confused. If you have difficulty choosing the correct word, look in your dictionary to see if there are examples of the right word and the wrong word used in sentences. Try to write your own sentences so that you can remember how to use the words correctly.

Choose the correct alternative from each pair.

Set 1

It is hypocritical to **1.** *moan/mourn* about the **2.** *damage/injury* being done to our environment unless we are prepared to do something about it. Everyone of us has a duty to keep our country tidy. Instead of leaving litter **3.** *laying/lying* around, we should put it in litter bins. It requires hardly any effort, yet it makes an **4.** *appreciable/appreciative* difference. Moreover, we should be made **5.** *conscientious/conscious* of the way the countryside is being spoilt and how it will **6.** *affect/effect* our future. We should refuse to **7.** *accept/except* the **8.** *assumption/presumption* that the **9.** *process/procession* is inevitable. Words on their own are **10.** *priceless/worthless*. Positive **11.** *action/activity* is required to **12.** *overcome/overtake* **13.** *inconsiderable/inconsiderate* attitudes and to bring about change. By **14.** *curing/treating* our surroundings more **15.** *respectably/respectfully*, we can do a lot to improve the **16.** *currant/current* state of affairs. **17.** *As far as/As long as* I'm concerned, the situation is **18.** *intolerable/intolerant* and it is regrettable that so many people close their eyes to the problem. One of the **19.** *principal/principle* dangers is apathy, the **20.** *consequences/sequences* of which could be disastrous.

Set 2

I **1.** *wander/wonder* if you've ever stopped **2.** *considering/to consider* the amount of time you spend **3.** *looking at/watching* television each day, or what people did before 'the box' was **4.** *discovered/invented*. **5.** *Weather/Whether* watching TV is time well spent is open to question. The quality of the programmes **6.** *leaves/lets* a lot to be desired. One of the **7.** *criticisms/objections* often levelled **8.** *at/to* television is that it's killing the art of conversation. As far as I'm concerned, I'd much rather spend an evening socialising with friends than sit glued to the box. However, I seem to be in the minority, **9.** *that/which* I think is a shame. What really **10.** *gets/lets* me down is the commercial **11.** *brakes/breaks*. In spite of the fact that I'm not a TV fan, I do enjoy going to the cinema. **12.** *However/Moreover*, with the arrival of video recorders, a lot of cinemas have now been closed down or converted into bingo halls.

34 Word partnerships – 4

Match each adjective on the left with a noun on the right. Use each word once only. Write your answers in the boxes.

Set 1

1.	faultless	**a.**	cruelty
2.	fearless	**b.**	driver
3.	harmless	**c.**	food
4.	hopeless	**d.**	fun
5.	priceless	**e.**	night
6.	reckless	**f.**	painting
7.	restless	**g.**	performance
8.	senseless	**h.**	rubbish
9.	tasteless	**i.**	situation
10.	worthless	**j.**	warrior

1	
2	
3	
4	
5	
6	
7	
8	
9	
10	

Set 2

Now do the same with these words.

1.	cheerful	**a.**	advice
2.	delightful	**b.**	answer
3.	frightful	**c.**	character
4.	harmful	**d.**	illness
5.	hopeful	**e.**	mess
6.	painful	**f.**	news
7.	restful	**g.**	night
8.	spiteful	**h.**	remarks
9.	truthful	**i.**	side-effects
10.	useful	**j.**	weather

1	
2	
3	
4	
5	
6	
7	
8	
9	
10	

Remember to choose the best, most natural partnerships.

35 Getting old

Choose the word or phrase which best completes each sentence. Give one answer only to each question:

1. As we get older it gets more difficult to keep up with the . . . .
   a. present **b.** times **c.** moment **d.** date
2. Elderly people are . . . . to forget things easily.
   a. art **b.** prone **c.** open **d.** prey
3. That song . . . . me of my youth.
   a. recalls **b.** remembers **c.** reminds **d.** recollects
4. You're too old to carry on working. It's time you called it a . . . .
   a. day **b.** week **c.** month **d.** year
5. He looks a great deal older. His worries seem to have taken a terrible . . . . on his health.
   a. burden **b.** strain **c.** tax **d.** toll
6. When you retire, you'll receive a(n) . . . . from the government.
   a. allowance **b.** benefit **c.** grant **d.** pension
7. Except for the . . . . cold and cough, I've been remarkably healthy all my life.
   a. irregular **b.** odd **c.** infrequent **d.** timely
8. Queen Victoria's death marked the end of an . . . .
   a. aria **b.** aura **c.** era **d.** area
9. Would you ever consider putting your parents in an old people's . . . . ?
   a. asylum **b.** home **c.** house **d.** hospital
10. I don't remember the fifties — they were before my . . . .
    a. age **b.** epoch **c.** period **d.** time
11. I've heard that joke before. It's as old as the . . . .
    a. hills **b.** history **c.** rocks **d.** times
12. The proportion of elderly people in the population is steadily . . . . as they live longer.
    a. falling **b.** growing up **c.** raising **d.** rising
13. Early retirement is a . . . . of reducing the workforce while avoiding redundancies.
    a. device **b.** means **c.** source **d.** proposal
14. Thinking about my childhood makes me feel very . . . .
    a. remembered **b.** memorable **c.** nostalgic **d.** reminiscent

36 Word formation — 2

Remember that when you look up a word, you can often build your vocabulary by seeing if you can form other words. Some nouns, for example, can be formed by adding **-ity** or **-ness** to an adjective. Sometimes changes in spelling are necessary, for example:

able	ability
happy	happiness

Can you think of any more examples?

Form a noun from the adjective given to complete the sentence.

1. There was a lot of . . . . outside his door. (ACTIVE)
2. After some time she recovered . . . . (CONSCIOUS)
3. His . . . . will lead to misfortune one day! (CURIOUS)
4. I don't expect such . . . . from my staff. (FAMILIAR)
5. Is there any . . . . to treat her so badly? (NECESSARY)
6. Her writing certainly shows . . . . (ORIGINAL)
7. There's a . . . . that he'll come tomorrow. (POSSIBLE)
8. This car is famous for its . . . . (RELIABLE)
9. This used to happen with alarming . . . . (REGULAR)
10. There was a look of . . . . on her face. (SAD)
11. He was unaware of the . . . . of her illness. (SERIOUS)
12. They were shocked by his lack of . . . . (SENSITIVE)
13. Any . . . . is purely coincidental. (SIMILAR)
14. He was impressed by the . . . . of her skin. (SMOOTH)
15. My . . . . is Italian sculpture. (SPECIAL)
16. I have a . . . . for sticky buns. (WEAK)

37 Choose the adverb

As you study English, notice how some adverbs form common partnerships with other words, for example:

They were **highly delighted**. He **sighed deeply**.

If you want to speak English in a natural way, you should note down and learn expressions like this. Word partnerships are an important part of natural English.

From the following list choose a suitable adverb to complete each sentence. Use each adverb once only.

distinctly	**greatly**	**openly**	**sorely**
entirely	**highly**	**passionately**	**unconditionally**
flatly	**incredibly**	**perfectly**	**unreservedly**
fully	**longingly**	**reluctantly**	**virtually**

1. The fog was so thick that it was .... impossible to see your hand in front of your face.
2. They built up a team of .... motivated sales people.
3. He .... denied having stolen the money.
4. To think he's ninety! He's .... fit for his age!
5. Make sure you're .... insured before you go.
6. He .... admitted that he was only in it for the money. I was surprised at his candour.
7. She was .... admired for her innovative ideas.
8. She made it .... clear that she wasn't satisfied.
9. He apologised .... for the trouble he had caused.
10. They gazed .... at the sports car in the show room.
11. She .... agreed to come despite her misgivings.
12. It's .... my fault. I take full responsibility.
13. The general said that they had to surrender .... — there was nothing to negotiate.
14. I'm .... tempted to have another of those cakes!
15. He's loved her .... ever since they first met.
16. There's nothing wrong with my hearing! I .... heard them say they would be here at 6 o'clock!

38 Sounds Funny

One kind of humour quite popular with English speakers is where phrases which sound the same can have two different meanings. One example of this is with the names of authors of books.
For example:

'Moving Home' by Ivor Newhouse
(I've a new house)

In this exercise you have to match each book title with its author. Use each author once only. Write your answers in the boxes.
If you can pronounce the author's name correctly you should get the joke!

1.	'The Explosion'	**a.**	by Anne O'Rack	**1**	
2.	'Drums And Trumpets'	**b.**	by C. Shaw	**2**	
3.	'Make Money Easily'	**c.**	by I. Malone	**3**	
4.	'Road Transport'	**d.**	by Dinah Mite	**4**	
5.	'Crime Prevention'	**e.**	by Carrie Mee	**5**	
6.	'Keep Trying'	**f.**	by Ivor Headache	**6**	
7.	'The Lady Artist'	**g.**	by Robin Banks	**7**	
8.	'Outdoor Clothes'	**h.**	by Ann Tarctic	**8**	
9.	'So Tired'	**i.**	by Laura Norder	**9**	
10.	'Jungle Fever'	**j.**	by Andrew Pictures	**10**	
11.	'At The South Pole'	**k.**	by Laurie Driver	**11**	
12.	'Solitude'	**l.**	by Maxie Mumm	**12**	
13.	'On The Beach'	**m.**	by Percy Vere	**13**	
14.	'Make The Most Of Life'	**n.**	by Amos Quito	**14**	

39 In the office

Use what you have around you to help yourself learn English. Look at the objects you find at work, school or home and ask yourself if you know how to say them in English. If not, find out and make a list of words connected with a certain place or occupation.

Put the name of the item under each picture. Choose from the following list. Use each word once only.

date stamp
guillotine
notepad
paper clips
pencil sharpener
punch
ruler
scales
scissors
stamps
stapler
staples
string
tray
wastepaper bin

1. . . . .

2. . . . .

3. . . . .

4. . . . .

5. . . . .

6. . . . .

7. . . . .

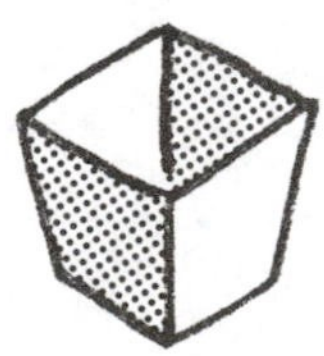

8. . . . .

9. . . . .

10. . . . .

11. . . . .

12. . . . .

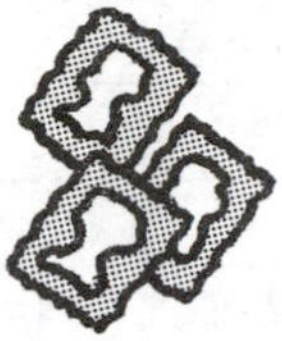

13. . . . .

14. . . . .

15. . . . .

Now use the correct words from the list to complete the sentences.

1. She used the . . . . to make holes in the paper.

2. They threw the rubbish into the . . . .

3. I need a . . . . to underline this phrase.

4. He wrote the message down in his . . . .

5. Put it on the . . . . and we'll see how heavy it is.

6. Will the . . . . be long enough to tie up this parcel?

7. If you want to cut paper use the . . . . , not scissors.

8. Could you put the letters in the . . . . on my desk, please.

40 Phrasal verbs — 2

Use the words on the left to make two-word verbs. Complete the table on the right to show the meaning of each verb.

1 LAY		2 LOOK		3 GET
	4 SORT		5 DROP	
6 DO		7 STICK		8 GO
	9 TURN		10 TAKE	
A UP		B OVER		C DOWN
	D ON		E OFF	
F OUT		G LIKE		H FOR
	I TO		J IN	

BE ATTRACTED TO	8	
FASTEN		A
KEEP TO	7	
LOWER THE VOLUME		C
MAKE PROGRESS	3	
MAKE REDUNDANT		E
RESEMBLE	2	
SOLVE		F
TAKE CONTROL OF	10	
VISIT		J

Use the phrasal verbs to complete each of these sentences:

1. I don't really . . . . Chinese food.

2. Were the workers given the sack or were they . . . . ?

3. You should do what you believe is right and . . . . your principles.

4. Why don't you . . . . on your way home from work?

5. I've got a problem and you can help me to . . . . it . . . .

6. I had to help the children . . . . their coats as they had trouble with their buttons.

7. Unless you . . . . the cassette player, the neighbours will start to complain.

8. I'm finding it difficult to . . . . with my work as I keep getting interruptions.

9. Don't you think she . . . . her mother?

10. Who's going to . . . . the business when the present owner retires?

41 Number idioms

Complete each sentence with one of the following words.
Some are used more than once.

eleventh	**nineteen**	**second**
first	**ninety-nine**	**sixth**
forty	**one**	**two**

1. At the . . . . hour they managed to get together enough money to buy the house.
2. I'm tired of playing . . . . fiddle to him! Why can't I take some of the decisions for a change?
3. She always talks . . . . to the dozen. You never have a chance to get a word in edgeways.
4. He was in . . . . minds about whether to go to the dance or not.
5. I wasn't going to go out but on . . . . thoughts I need some fresh air.
6. He's gone upstairs to have . . . . winks after all his exertions.
7. The service in that shop is . . . . to none.
8. Some . . . . sense made her look up as he pulled out his gun.
9. Changing nappies has become . . . . nature to me since my son was born.
10. . . . . times out of a hundred you can arrive late and he won't notice, but today had to be my unlucky day!
11. I don't believe in love at . . . . sight. You've got to get to know people.
12. He's back to square . . . . now that they've turned down his application.
13. She came off . . . . best in the argument.
14. They don't know the . . . . thing about running this kind of business.
15. As he had a car, he was . . . . up on me when it came to inviting girls out.

Now underline all the special expressions which contain a number. Remember to add word partnerships, as well as new words to your English.

42 Complete the word

Use each definition to complete the word beginning with 'com'.

state of deep unconsciousness COM
funny COM
usual COM
order COM
express annoyance COM
group of people living together COM
totally COM
small room in railway carriage COM
something adding new difficulties COM
including everything essential COM
understandable COM
showing sympathy COM
payment for inconvenience or loss COM
pass on information COM
give a commentary COM
a lot of noise and confusion COM
start (verb) COM
business organisation COM
force (verb) COM
, COM
thing used to tidy hair COM

43 Word partnerships – 5

Complete the adjectives in each set by using the correct letter.
In addition, form the opposite by using the correct prefix. The prefix will be one of the following:

il-, im-, in-, ir- or **un-**

Finally, match the adjective formed with a suitable noun. Use each word once only. Write your answer in the space provided.

Set 1

attain ble	*insurmountable*	difficulties
compat ble	....	goal
leg ble	....	handwriting
palat ble	....	lifestyles
reli ble	....	source
surmount ble	....	suggestion

Set 2

access ble	....	decision
admiss ble	....	evidence
bear ble	....	heat
envi ble	....	reputation
print ble	....	place
revers ble	....	story

Set 3

cur ble	....	action
defens ble	....	component
hospit ble	....	disease
plaus ble	....	environment
profit ble	....	explanation
replace ble	....	meeting

44 Business world

Choose the word or phrase which best completes each sentence. Give one answer only to each question:

1. Due to a fall in demand, a number of workers in the factory were made . . . .
   a. obsolete **b.** unemployed **c.** redundant **d.** lay-offs
2. There's no . . . . in applying for the job unless you have the right qualifications.
   a. point **b.** reason **c.** use **d.** worth
3. If you . . . . in turning up late for work, I will have no alternative but to ask you to leave.
   a. desist **b.** insist **c.** persist **d.** resist

4. The job requires a good . . . . for figures.
   a. head **b.** understanding **c.** brain **d.** faculty
5. The government has been heavily . . . . for failing to reduce unemployment.
   a. charged **b.** accused **c.** criticised **d.** told off
6. Being a manager entails . . . . responsibility to other members of staff.
   a. deploying **b.** commissioning **c.** delegating **d.** nominating
7. It makes sense to . . . . a proportion of your profits back into the business.
   a. plant **b.** plough **c.** sow **d.** reap
8. The boss . . . . to his secretary using the office phone for personal calls.
   a. disapproves **b.** criticises **c.** disagrees **d.** objects

9. I decided to take a part-time degree with .... applying for a better job.
a. the intention to **b.** a view to **c.** the purpose to **d.** an aim to

10. As I won't be able to attend the meeting, I'd like you to sign ....
a. on my place **b.** on my behalf **c.** on my name **d.** on my account

11. The amount of tax you pay is .... to your income.
a. based **b.** assessed **c.** measured **d.** proportionate

12. The disagreement between the management and the union led to a ....
a. sidestep **b.** walk-out **c.** sidewalk **d.** walkover

13. Skilled workers can .... high wages.
a. command **b.** insist **c.** order **d.** required

14. I've decided to .... handing in my notice until I can find something better.
a. call off **b.** bring off **c.** put off **d.** take off

15. If you want to make a good impression, it's important to .... your colleagues.
a. keep away from **b.** keep in with **c.** keep out of **d.** keep on at

16. Although we haven't made much of a profit this year, there's a strong .... of business improving.
a. horizon **b.** prospect **c.** project **d.** perspective

17. The new productivity agreement should lead to an increase in ....
a. outlook **b.** outcome **c.** output **d.** outline

18. If certain industries didn't receive a .... from the State, they'd stand little chance of surviving.
a. donation **b.** mortgage **c.** credit **d.** subsidy

45 Product information

You don't have to be in an English-speaking country to see real English. It is usually possible to buy an English newspaper or magazine or even get one sent to you. The advertisements in them can be very useful in helping you build up lists of words used when talking about different products.

In this exercise you will see some information about a product. You must decide which product is being referred to. Choose the product from the following list. Each product is referred to once only.

bathroom cabinet	**bath mat**	**garden hose**	**iron**
bathroom scales	**camera**	**sewing machine**	**shower**
electric fan	**petrol can**	**tennis racket**	**tent**
electric toaster	**train set**	**video recorder**	**watch**

Twin mirrored sliding doors and interior shelf over open display shelf.

1. ....

Includes lights, buffet car, ten figures, luggage, platform and track.

2. ....

White resin strap and dark blue dial

3. ....

White sides. Variable browning control. Easy clean crumb tray.

4. ....

Moulded suckers on underside. Machine washable. Co-ordinates with shower curtain.

5. ....

8kW. Fully stabilized to maintain a safe and comfortable pressure even when water pressure fluctuates.

6. ....

Graphite/glass-fibre frame. Synthetic stringing. Synthetic grip. Mid size head.

f3.5/35mm lens. Auto focus. Motor advance.

7. ....

8. ....

3 automatic stitches plus manual embroidery, domino, oval, triangular.

Complete with tap connector and spray nozzle with easy shut-off facility.

9. ....

10. ....

Picture search at 9 times normal speed. Time overlap warning indicator.

Sewn-in ground sheet. Comes complete with steel ridge pole and uprights, pegs.

11. ....

12. ....

Thermostat control. Variable steam control graded 1-6. Unique, removable anti-scaling device.

Capacity 10 litre.

13. ....

14. ....

Cork mat. Calibrated to 19 stone and 120 kg.

3-speed push button control. 12 inchblade. Adjustable tilt.

15. ....

16. ....

46 Word partnerships – 6

Match each word on the left with a noun on the right. Use each word once only. Write your answers in the boxes.

Set 1

1.	capital	**a.**	appointment
2.	clerical	**b.**	argument
3.	exact	**c.**	commitment
4.	fierce	**d.**	entertainment
5.	financial	**e.**	judgement
6.	impartial	**f.**	measurements
7.	monthly	**g.**	punishment
8.	popular	**h.**	repayments
9.	special	**i.**	requirements
10.	total	**j.**	settlement

1	
2	
3	
4	
5	
6	
7	
8	
9	
10	

Set 2

Now do the same with these words.

1.	advertising	**a.**	advisor
2.	conscientious	**b.**	appliance
3.	domestic	**c.**	cabinet
4.	filing	**d.**	campaign
5.	financial	**e.**	effect
6.	greenhouse	**f.**	interest
7.	minority	**g.**	objector
8.	passive	**h.**	party
9.	political	**i.**	resistance
10.	public	**j.**	transport

1	
2	
3	
6	
4	
5	
7	
8	
9	
10	

47 Horrible joke time

Different people find different things funny.
Here are some examples of jokes which some people find quite amusing.
(Other people think they are just silly.)
Match the question on the left with the answer on the right.

1. If you had sixteen cows and two goats, what would you have?
2. What doesn't ask questions but must be answered?
3. What follows a dog everywhere?
4. What do you serve but never eat?
5. Why does a bull have horns?
6. Which is faster — heat or cold?
7. What must you pay when you go to school?
8. When a lemon asks for help, what does it want?
9. Why is a river rich?
10. Did your sister help you with your homework?
11. What gets wetter as it dries?
12. Doctor, I think I'm getting smaller. What should I do?
13. What do you get after it's been taken?
14. What's the best way to speak to a monster?
15. What kind of driver can't drive?

a. A tennis ball.
b. Your photograph.
c. Attention.
d. Heat. You can catch a cold.
e. A lot of milk.
f. A towel.
g. Lemonade
h. A screwdriver.
i. A telephone.
j. From a long distance!
k. Its tail.
l. No, sir. She did all of it.
m. Because its bell doesn't work.
n. You'll have to be a little patient.
o. Because it has two banks.

Write your answers here:

1	2	3	4	5	6	7	8	9	10	11	12	13	14	15

48 Studies and exams

Choose the word or phrase which best completes each sentence. Give one answer only to each question:

1. Being quick on the . . . . the students made rapid progress.
a. intake **b.** take-off **c.** uptake **d.** takeover

2. I was so absorbed in the book I was reading that I completely lost . . . . of the time.
a. count **b.** touch **c.** sight **d.** track

3. You'll have to work hard to . . . . the rest of the class as they started studying before you.
a. hold on to **b.** catch up with **c.** keep on at **d.** reach out with

4. . . . . you read the instructions carefully, you'll understand what to do.
a. As far as **b.** Provided **c.** As much as **d.** As well as

5. You'll just have to learn these expressions . . . .
a. by word **b.** to heart **c.** by heart **d.** with all your heart

6. As a result of all the hard work they put in, the students reached a high . . . . of achievement.
a. level **b.** note **c.** grade **d.** mark

7. I don't seem to be making any progress and it's beginning to . . . . me down.
a. carry **b.** get **c.** pull **d.** take

8. . . . . a week goes by without the teacher giving us a test.
a. Infrequently **b.** Hardly **c.** Practically **d.** No sooner

9. Your failure can be .... to the fact that you didn't do any work.
a. attributed **b.** accused **c.** blamed **d.** explained

10. You'll have to be strict with that class of children as they quickly get ....
a. on hand **b.** in hand **c.** out of hand **d.** by hand

11. At this time of the year the number of students in the school tends to ....
a. dwindle **b.** deteriorate **c.** reduce **d.** lessen

12. Before the end of the course you'll be given a .... exam to prepare you for the real thing.
a. fake **b.** mock **c.** false **d.** trial

13. She's .... stupid — she's just lazy.
a. by no means **b.** by no degree **c.** by no extent **d.** by no way

14. How are you .... your studies? Do you feel that you're making headway?
a. getting down to **b.** getting ahead of
c. getting on with **d.** getting up to

15. Do university students receive a(n) .... from the State in your country?
a. allowance **b.** grant **c.** pension **d.** income

16. Unless you pull your socks up, you've got no .... of passing the exam.
a. chance **b.** possibility **c.** likelihood **d.** probability

17. The candidate .... nervously up and down waiting to be called for the interview.
a. marched **b.** paced **c.** strutted **d.** plodded

18. You should start revising for your exam as soon as possible. Any delay will result in .... time being lost.
a. conclusive **b.** vital **c.** priceless **d.** invaluable

49 Animal world

Match the noun on the left with a verb on the right.
Use each word once only.

1.	a bee	**a.**	barks
2.	a bird	**b.**	bleats
3.	a cat	**c.**	buzzes
4.	a dog	**d.**	clucks
5.	a duck	**e.**	croaks
6.	a frog	**f.**	grunts
7.	a hen	**g.**	hisses
8.	a horse	**h.**	hoots
9.	a lion	**i.**	mews
10.	an owl	**j.**	neighs
11.	a pig	**k.**	quacks
12.	a sheep	**l.**	roars
13.	a snake	**m.**	twitters

1	
2	
3	
4	
5	
6	
7	
8	
9	
10	
11	
12	
13	

Use one of the following words to complete each sentence.
Use each word once only.

galloped **hopped** **prowled** **slithered** **swooped**

14. The snake .... under a rock.

15. The horse .... along the beach.

16. The frog .... on to another stone.

17. That lion .... around our camp again last night.

18. The seagulls .... down from the sky.

50 Opposites – adjectives

Remember that the opposite of a word depends on its context. That is why it is important to learn new words in sentences.

Complete each sentence with the opposite of the word in brackets. Choose from one of the following words. Use each word once only.

approximate	**crude**	**even**	**harmful**
clear	**delicate**	**flexible**	**reluctant**
compulsory	**dim**	**graceful**	**scarce**
considerable	**easy**	**guilty**	**superficial**

1. They gave me .... instructions. (AMBIGUOUS)
2. This machine is very .... to use. (AWKWARD)
3. She moved in a very .... way. (AWKWARD)
4. This kind of activity can be .... (BENEFICIAL)
5. She noted down the .... time of departure. (EXACT)
6. I'm sure he was .... of the charge. (INNOCENT)
7. These houses all have .... numbers. (ODD)
8. Food was .... in that region. (PLENTIFUL)
9. He has a .... knowledge of the government's economic policy. (PROFOUND)
10. I have a fairly .... schedule. (RIGID)
11. There's a .... difference between the two. (SLIGHT)
12. The bomb had a .... timing device. (SOPHISTICATED)
13. This sauce has a very .... flavour. (STRONG)
14. The light was so .... that I couldn't make out who was speaking. (STRONG)
15. We had 25 .... redundancies last year. (VOLUNTARY)
16. He was very .... to take part. (WILLING)

Can you think of any more opposites for the adjectives for when they are used in different contexts?

51 Body idioms — 2

Complete each sentence with the correct part of the body.
Choose from the following words. Some are used more than once.

arms	**fingers**	**hands**	**neck**
back	**feet**	**head**	**nose**
eyes	**foot**	**heart**	**teeth**
face	**hand**	**legs**	**tongue**

1. I'm fed up to the back . . . . with all these complaints!

2. They managed to get the upper . . . . and gain control of the company.

3. He looked so ridiculous that it was hard to keep a straight . . . .

4. I got off on the wrong . . . . by arriving late for the interview.

5. He looked down his . . . . at people who earned a lower salary than he did.

6. The car changed . . . . at a good price.

7. I can't turn my . . . . on her now that she's in so much trouble.

8. He didn't want to lose . . . . by admitting he had made a mistake.

9. You must never set . . . . in there again!

10. I've got my . . . . full at the moment but I'll be able to help you next month.

11. Let's go for a walk to stretch our . . . .

12. He can't have been serious! Are you sure he didn't have his . . . . in his cheek when he said it?

13. I'm going to stick my . . . . out and say the weekend will be a great success.

14. She may seem a bit frightening but her . . . . is in the right place.

15. I'm afraid the wine went to my . . . . and I made rather a fool of myself.

16. The meeting got out of . . . . and they had to call the police.

17. She got cold . . . . when she realised how difficult it would be, and tried to get out of doing it.

18. Let's keep our . . . . crossed that the weather will be better tomorrow.

19. We had to pay through the . . . . to get a hotel room as we had arrived at a busy time.

20. She didn't exactly welcome her daughter-in-law with open . . . .

21. I wish he wouldn't poke his . . . . into other people's business.

22. In his mother's . . . . , he can do no wrong.

23. I'm happy that our daughter's education is in such good . . . .

24. I can't make . . . . nor tail of this exercise.

52 Word partnerships – 7

Match the verb on the left with a noun on the right. Use each word once only. Write your answers in the boxes.

Set 1

1.	broaden	**a.**	the blow
2.	deaden	**b.**	your hair
3.	fasten	**c.**	your life
4.	sharpen	**d.**	your mind
5.	shorten	**e.**	the pain
6.	soften	**f.**	a pencil
7.	straighten	**g.**	a relationship
8.	strengthen	**h.**	your seat belt
9.	sweeten	**i.**	a screw
10.	tighten	**j.**	the taste

1	
2	
3	
4	
5	
6	
7	
8	
9	
10	

Set 2

Now do the same with these words.

1.	amplify	**a.**	your actions
2.	clarify	**b.**	the authorities
3.	justify	**c.**	the demonstrators
4.	magnify	**d.**	the evidence
5.	modify	**e.**	your plans
6.	notify	**f.**	your requirements
7.	pacify	**g.**	a situation
8.	purify	**h.**	a slide
9.	specify	**i.**	sound
10.	verify	**j.**	water

1	
2	
3	
4	
5	
6	
7	
8	
9	
10	

53 Expressions with 'in'

Here are some expressions with 'in'. Make sure you understand them before doing the exercise.

in agreement	**in charge of**	**in comparison with**	**in demand**
in the end	**in the lead**	**in fact**	**in favour of**
in general	**in a hurry**	**in motion**	**in a position to**
in private	**in silence**	**in tears**	**in a whisper**

Put the correct words from the above list into the following sentences. Use each expression once only.

1. Who is in . . . . that group of students?
2. They're in . . . . the idea but I'm against it.
3. She looks as if she's about 50 but in . . . . she's over 60.
4. We saw her in . . . . so we tried to cheer her up.
5. They listened to him in . . . . Nobody said a word.
6. This rain means umbrellas are very much in . . . .
7. Slow down! You're always in . . . . !
8. Do not get off while the bus is still in . . . .
9. At the moment Helen is in . . . . and Ruth is second.
10. Can we talk in . . . . ? Somebody might overhear us.
11. She could only speak in . . . . because of her sore throat.
12. As we're all in . . . . , we can sign the contract.
13. My hair is quite short in . . . . my sister's.
14. I'm afraid I'm not in . . . . to help at present.
15. In . . . . we understood what he was trying to tell us but it certainly took a long time!
16. I like music in . . . . and jazz in particular.

Once again you see how important word partnerships are!

54 Stress: noun and verb

Remember to keep checking the stress patterns of words as you can cause confusion if you get this wrong.

Some words have the stress on a different syllable depending on whether they are a noun or a verb, for example:

import (noun) im**port** (verb)

Most words, however, do not change their stress but it is important to know which syllable the stress is on.

In this exercise you must put the words into three lists corresponding to their stress pattern.
Remember to check any words you are not sure about.

answer	**display**	**present**	**subject**
attempt	**favour**	**produce**	**support**
comfort	**gossip**	**question**	**suspect**
conduct	**honour**	**rebel**	**transport**
control	**increase**	**record**	**treasure**
convict	**mistake**	**regard**	**visit**
decay	**parade**	**regret**	
defeat	**picture**	**shower**	

1. Stress on the first syllable	2. Stress on the second syllable	3. Variable stress
....	....	....
....	....	....
....	....	....
....	....	....
....	....	....
....	....	....
....	....	....
....	....	....
....	....	....
....	....	....

55 Word partnerships – 8

Match each adjective on the left with a noun on the right. Use each word once only. Write your answers in the boxes.

Set 1

1.	courageous	**a.**	achievement
2.	dangerous	**b.**	behaviour
3.	horrendous	**c.**	ceremony
4.	infectious	**d.**	deeds
5.	industrious	**e.**	disaster
6.	luxurious	**f.**	disease
7.	nutritious	**g.**	drugs
8.	outrageous	**h.**	food
9.	religious	**i.**	student
10.	tremendous	**j.**	surroundings

1	
2	
3	
4	
5	
6	
7	
8	
9	
10	

Set 2

Now do the same with these words.

1.	enviable	**a.**	clothes
2.	fashionable	**b.**	disease
3.	foreseeable	**c.**	future
4.	incurable	**d.**	neighbours
5.	interminable	**e.**	position
6.	portable	**f.**	request
7.	sociable	**g.**	television
8.	unbeatable	**h.**	urge
9.	uncontrollable	**i.**	value
10.	unreasonable	**j.**	wait

1	
2	
3	
4	
5	
6	
7	
8	
9	
10	

Now write some sentences of your own using some of the word partnerships.

56 Crime and punishment

Choose the word or phrase which best completes each sentence. Give one answer only to each question:

1. The judge . . . . the murderer to life imprisonment.
   a. prosecuted **b.** sentenced **c.** convicted **d.** accused

2. You shouldn't take the law . . . . your own hands — there's a proper way of going about things.
   a. by **b.** into **c.** under **d.** with
3. Capital punishment is supposed to act as a . . . .
   a. deterrent **b.** safeguard **c.** prevention **d.** distraction
4. It took the jury a long time to reach a . . . .
   a. summary **b.** conviction **c.** sentence **d.** verdict
5. I don't know whether you're . . . . or telling the truth.
   a. deluding **b.** intriguing **c.** bluffing **d.** deceiving
6. Money is said to be the . . . . of all evil.
   a. source **b.** reason **c.** cause **d.** root
7. You should be . . . . when strangers call at the door and ask to see some form of identification.
   a. weary **b.** choosy **c.** wary **d.** particular
8. If you're caught exceeding the speed limit, you'll have to pay a(n) . . . .
   a. indemnity **b.** penalty **c.** fine **d.** price

9. Instead of being sent to prison, the shoplifter was........ with a fine.
a. let away **b.** let off **c.** let loose **d.** let out

10. The judge .... the case because there wasn't a scrap of evidence to prove the suspect's guilt.
a. disallowed **b.** dismissed **c.** abandoned **d.** disqualified

11. I was so desperate for money to pay off my debts that I........ to embezzlement.
a. resisted **b.** resorted **c.** retaliated **d.** retorted

12. Poverty frequently .... people to crime.
a. brings **b.** compels **c.** drives **d.** induces

13. The Embassy was .... after a bomb warning was received.
a. abandoned **b.** evacuated **c.** evicted **d.** expelled

14. They .... me for causing the accident although it wasn't my fault.
a. acquitted **b.** blamed **c.** charged **d.** announced

15. The policeman was .... to have accepted a bribe.
a. affirmed **b.** alleged **c.** accused **d.** announced

16. The police car sped after the robbers with its .... blaring.
a. siren **b.** gong **c.** bell **d.** alarm

17. The pickpocket .... having stolen the old lady's purse.
a. defied **b.** refused **c.** denied **d.** rejected

18. The demonstrators carried banners with .... criticising the police.
a. mottos **b.** inscriptions **c.** slogans **d.** notices

57 Confusing words — 3

It doesn't matter if you make mistakes when you're using English — that's how you learn. However, it does matter if you keep on making the same mistakes. Look back at the exercises in this book which you have found difficult. Are you sure you know how to use the words correctly now? If not, write sentences using the words you aren't sure about.

Choose the correct alternative from each pair.

Set 1

As **1.** *far / long* as you're not **2.** *adverse / averse* to the hustle and **3.** *bustle / rustle* of crowds, I suggest you **4.** *pay / spend* a visit to Portobello Road. It's a street market where you can find everything under the **5.** *sky / sun*. **6.** *However / Moreover*, you should be **7.** *wary / weary* of pickpockets as tourists are their **8.** *bread and butter / bread and jam*. The most **9.** *sensible / sensitive* **10.** *coarse / course* of **11.** *action / activity* is to leave all your valuables at home. You can haggle over the price of items such as antiques or second-hand clothing, and, if you're careful, you can pick up some real bargains. **12.** *Moreover / Nevertheless*, you have to be on your guard, or you may end up with **13.** *priceless / worthless* junk. Examine the goods carefully before you part with your money to **14.** *assure / ensure* that you don't regret your extravagance later.

Set 2

The **1.** *advice / advise* of friends can often prove to be **2.** *invaluable / valueless* when we have difficulties to face. Even though they are unable to solve problems for us, their support can help to **3.** *raise / rise* our spirits and they can cheer us up when we're feeling **4.** *depressed / depressing*. They **5.** *remember / remind* us of the fact that we're not alone and we should be **6.** *appreciable / appreciative* of what they have to offer. Of course, we should not be dependent on others. We're all ultimately responsible for our own **7.** *actions / activities* and we all have to **8.** *accept / agree* the consequences of the **9.** *faults / mistakes* we make. However, there's a **10.** *distinct / distinctive* difference between leaning on others and being prepared to listen to what they have to **11.** *say / tell*. Friends can often **12.** *avoid / prevent* us from seeing things in a distorted way and help us to **13.** *bare / bear* the hardships that lie ahead. It is **14.** *intolerable / intolerant* if we have nobody to talk to and have no **15.** *alteration / alternative* but to bottle up our feelings. We all need to give, and to receive, friendship. It helps to make us human.

58 Moods

Remember that organising the words you learn into categories can help you to build your vocabulary. If you read a newspaper article, for example, where people are angry or frightened about something, see how many different words you can find to express these feelings. Whenever you find new words or expressions, note them down in a sentence.

Put each of these adjectives in the correct column according to the type of mood it describes.

annoyed	**delighted**	**grumpy**	**overjoyed**
apprehensive	**depressed**	**heartbroken**	**petrified**
cheerful	**despondent**	**infuriated**	**relieved**
contented	**exhilarated**	**intimidated**	**scared**
cross	**furious**	**irate**	**startled**
dejected	**gloomy**	**miserable**	**terrified**

1. ANGRY

....

....

....

....

....

....

2. FRIGHTENED

....

....

....

....

....

....

3. HAPPY

....

....

....

....

....

....

4. UNHAPPY

....

....

....

....

....

....

To help you remember any new words you have seen, use each one in a sentence.

59 Word formation — 3

When you look up a word in a dictionary, see if you can form any other words from it. Sometimes these words will be included in the definiton of the word and sometimes they will appear separately. Look before and after each dictionary entry to see what words you can find formed from the same source.

Complete each sentence with the correct form of the word in brackets. In some cases you will also have to use a prefix. This will be either **dis-**, **im-**, **ir-**, **mis-**, **non-** or **un-**.

Set 1

1. He's so ....! No wonder he has no friends! (AGREE)
2. We must meet soon, ... before Saturday. (PREFER)
3. The earthquake caused .... damage. (EXTEND)
4. The roads were .... because of the snow. (PASS)
5. This place has changed beyond .... (RECOGNISE)
6. She took the job to be .... independent. (FINANCE)
7. He died under .... circumstances. (SUSPECT)
8. We can look forward to a period of .... (PROSPER)
9. I'm afraid this plan will prove very .... (DIVIDE)
10. They were caught in an............. shower of rain. (EXPECT)
11. I'm afraid I rather .... agreed to help. (WISE)
12. She spent hours getting the house .... clean. (SPOT)

Set 2

1. If I were you, I wouldn't make a .... just yet. (DECIDE)
2. It's .... of motorists to drink and drive. (RESPONSE)
3. If you have any special ...., please let me know. (REQUIRE)
4. I don't mind .... criticism but there's no need to be unpleasant. (CONSTRUCT)

5. If you're not too busy, I could do with some . . . . (ASSIST)

6. I had my trousers . . . . because they were too short. (LONG)

7. If you lose your cheque book, you should . . . . the bank without delay. (NOTE)

8. It was a . . . . letter addressed to the boss and the secretary shouldn't have opened it. (CONFIDE)

9. The . . . . of the flight was delayed so we had to spend the night at the airport. (DEPART)

10. The teacher warned the children that if they . . . . again, they'd be punished. (BEHAVE)

11. It's . . . . to study a language if you're never going to use it. (POINT)

12. I'm afraid I'm in the . . . . position of being out of work and heavily in debt. (ENVY)

Set 3

1. Great works of art like the Mona Lisa are . . . . (PRICE)

2. I'm afraid you've . . . . me because that's not what I meant. (UNDERSTAND)

3. Why do we always end up by having an . . . . ? (ARGUE)

4. I've been a . . . . since I had a heart attack. (SMOKE)

5. Unless you . . . . , I won't forgive you. (APOLOGY)

6. I wish you'd be . . . . instead of telling me lies. (TRUE)

7. The weather in this country is so . . . . that you never know what to expect. (PREDICT)

8. It's a . . . . doing business with you. (PLEASE)

9. Although the stone in your ring looks like a diamond, I'm afraid it's . . . . (WORTH)

10. How can you . . . . the fact that some people live in mansions while others live in slums? (JUST)

11. It's . . . . to expect to get something for nothing. (REASON)

12. If you're hoping to make a good . . . . , you should pay more . . . . to your . . . . (IMPRESS/ATTEND/APPEAR)

60 Expressing attitudes

Set 1

Complete the following using these adjectives:

keen sorry enthusiastic crazy typical good capable fed up

1. I suppose I'll just have to accept the job.
   >Well, you don't seem very . . . . about it.
2. I'm better at figures than you are. Let me add the bill up.
   >I'm quite . . . . of doing it myself, thank you.
3. He tries hard but he never seems to have much luck, does he?
   >I know what you mean. I feel a bit . . . . for him really.
4. Don't you mind him turning up late every morning?
   >Well, to tell you the truth, I am getting a bit . . . . with him.
5. Why did we agree to go to the Bengal Tiger for Jack's birthday? I don't even like Indian food!
   >No, I'm not very . . . . on it myself either.
6. Why don't you get out and meet people a bit more?
   >I'm afraid I'm not very . . . . at socialising.
7. Do you think she likes me?
   >Likes you? You must be blind! She's absolutely . . . . about you!
8. She didn't even say thank you for that bracelet I gave her!
   >Well, that's . . . . of her, isn't it?

Set 2

Complete these conversations using the following adjectives:

fond excited guilty scared mad sick

1. I suppose they'll end up sending me somewhere like Paris or Vienna.
   >Well, I must say, you don't sound very . . . . about it.
2. I don't really want us to have to go and live in London.
   >No, I'm not . . . . about the idea myself.
3. You give me the impression you don't like cats very much!
   >Rubbish, I'm quite . . . . of them actually.
4. Why don't you come clean with your boss and say you won't go to Karachi?
   >Well, to tell you the truth, I'm a bit . . . . of her. It's her temper!
5. The car won't start again!
   >Let's get rid of it. I'm . . . . of the damn thing!
6. She's written you dozens of letters and you've never once replied.
   >I know. I do feel a bit . . . . about it.

61 Phrasal verbs — 3

Use the words on the left to make two-word verbs. Complete the table on the right to show the meaning of each verb.

1 SIT		2 KEEP		3 PUT
	4 BREAK		5 RUN	
6 GO		7 TRY		8 STAND
	9 FIX		10 GET	
A BY		B OVER		C ON
	D BACK		E OUT	
F AWAY		G UP		H AFTER
	I OFF		J DOWN	

ARRANGE	9	
CHASE		H
CONTINUE	2	
ESCAPE		F
POSTPONE	3	
RELAX		D
EXPLAIN AGAIN	6	
STOP WORKING		J
SUPPORT	8	
TEST		E

Use the phrasal verbs to complete each of these sentences:

1. Have you . . . . an appointment yet?

2. If you . . . . smoking, you'll damage your health.

3. I'm afraid I'll have to . . . . the meeting until next week.

4. Could you . . . . the instructions again, please?

5. I can't decide whether to buy the machine or not until I've . . . . . . it . . . .

6. A good friend will always . . . . you no matter what you do.

7. If the car . . . . , we'll have to walk.

8. I can't . . . . and have a good time while there's still work to be done.

9. & **10.** The police . . . . the bank robbers but they managed to . . . .

62 Classified ads

Below you will see the first parts of some advertisements. Decide which classification each one should appear under.
Use each classification only once.

ANIMALS AND PETS	**COLLECTING**	**MUSIC**
ARTS & CRAFTS	**DO IT YOURSELF**	**OFFICE EQUIPMENT**
AUDIO & TV	**HOUSES FOR SALE**	**PHOTOGRAPHY**
CAMPING	**LAND**	**SAILING AND BOATING**

30 ft Dutch-built motor cruiser, 4 berths

1. . . . .

AERIAL BOOSTERS improves weak reception.

2. . . . .

AQUARIUMS direct from manufacturer

3. . . . .

GROUNDSHEETS 100% waterproof. Blue, brown or green.

4. . . . .

Corrugated fibre-glass roofing sheets, ideal for all those

5. . . . .

BEST PRICES PAID for autographed photos, letters of famous people

6. . . . .

ARE YOU OVER 65? Then why not retire to a bungalow by the sea?

7. . . . .

STRINGED INSTRUMENTS urgently required by leading

8. . . . .

PICTURE FRAMING made easy. Buy direct from the manufacturer.

9. . . . .

FOR SALE remote-control slide projector, excellent condition

10. . . . .

BUILDING PLOT quiet area, with planning permission for

11. . . . .

J.F. SUPPLIES for answering machines, call diverters,

12. . . . .

63 Colour idioms

Complete each sentence with the correct colour.

1. He saw . . . . when his son broke the window.
2. He got the . . . . light from his boss to carry out his plan.
3. Where did you get that . . . . eye? Have you been fighting again?
4. I'll believe it when I see it in . . . . and white.
5. She can't write any more cheques or her account will be in the . . . .
6. She told a . . . . lie to avoid hurting his feelings.
7. The invitation arrived out of the . . . .
8. He gave me a . . . . look when I mentioned payment.
9. The manager decided to show . . . . films in an attempt to lure people back to the cinema.
10. He painted the town . . . . to celebrate winning.
11. He was the . . . . sheep of the family and they rarely talked about him.
12. She bought these goods on the . . . . market.
13. There's so much . . . . tape if you want to get a work permit in this country!
14. He was . . . . with envy when they bought a new car.
15. The disco had a . . . . list of people who were to be refused entry.
16. They may be forced to build houses in the . . . . belt because the population is growing so fast.
17. We shall definitely roll out the . . . . carpet if he ever visits us.
18. A power failure could . . . . out an area of over 400 square kilometres.

64 Understatement

In English – as in many other languages – it is sometimes important not to say exactly what you mean, but to say it in a 'weaker' way – perhaps less direct or less strong. Match up what you say with what you are actually thinking:

Set 1

What you say:

1. Perhaps I'm not making myself very clear.
2. You don't have any trouble . finding things to talk about.
3. He's not my favourite person
4. Classical music's not really my scene.
5. It's not exactly ideal, is it?
6. He's not very nice to his wife.
7. It may be a little out of our price range.
8. We don't seem to be getting very far.

What you are thinking:

a. I hate classical music!
b. He's horrible to his wife!
c. We obviously can't afford it!
d. We're getting nowhere!
e. You never shut up!
f. I can't stand him!
g. It's totally unsuitable!
h. Why can't you understand me!

1		2		3		4		5		6		7		8	

Set 2

What you say:

1. I wouldn't mind having my book back when you have finished with it.
2. I think he'd had a bit too much to drink.
3. Statistics isn't really your . thing, is it?
4. I'd appreciate it if you could let me have the money soon.
5. Isn't it a bit on the small side?
6. I'm afraid I don't quite follow
7. I think you may have made a bit of a mess of it.
8. She's not exactly the best actress I've ever seen.

What you are thinking:

a. It's far too small!
b. She's a terrible actress!
c. You've ruined it!
d. He was blind drunk!
e. I want my book back!
f. What ARE you talking about?
g. You don't understand the first thing about statistics!
h. Pay up!

1		2		3		4		5		6		7		8	

Set 3

British people sometimes understate things even when they are being positive. Match up what they say with what they mean. Don't take these examples too seriously!

What you say:

1. It wasn't bad.
2. She's quite good-looking.
3. I think I could do with a holiday.
4. I'm quite pleased.
5. I'm a fairly reasonable tennis player.
6. It's not as easy as it looks.
7. You'll soon get the hang of it.
8. Try not to worry too much.
9. Things could be worse.
10. I did quite well in the exam.
11. He's getting on a bit.
12. It was rather warm.

What you are thinking:

a. I'm absolutely over the moon.
b. The Sahara comes to mind.
c. . . . . but not much worse.
d. It'll take you years to learn.
e. It's virtually impossible.
f. His son is 75!
g. She's devastatingly attractive.
h. I came first in the exam.
i. I'm utterly exhausted.
j. It was excellent.
k. I'd start looking for a new job!
l. I once got to the quarter-finals at Wimbledon.

1	2	3	4	5	6	7	8	9	10	11	12

Remember you can use some of these fixed expressions to make your own English more natural and friendly.

65 Expressions with 'That's'

Set 1

Look at these expressions. Each of them is a fixed expression you could use if you were involved in a discussion and there were a number of disagreements of different kinds.

1. That's beside the point.
2. That's not what I said at all.
3. That's hardly my fault!
4. That's nothing to do with me.
5. That's a ridiculous suggestion.
6. That's not quite what I meant.
7. That's taking things too far.
8. That's my whole point.
9. That's not the point.

Match each of those expressions to one of these meanings:

a. You have slightly misunderstood what I suggested.
b. I refuse to accept responsibility for that.
c. Don't blame me!
d. Don't introduce an irrelevant detail.
e. You are over-reacting or exaggerating.
f. I am annoyed because you are misrepresenting my ideas.
g. You've missed the most essential bit of the argument.
h. I am so annoyed by your suggestion that I'm rejecting it.
i. At last you've understood what I've been saying.

1	2	3	4	5	6	7	8	9

Set 2

Now match each of these expressions with the explanations:

1. That's taking things too far.
2. That's very kind of you.
3. That's the best I can do.
4. That's that.

a. I've tried to help – don't ask for more.
b. We've finished!
c. You're over-reacting.
d. I'm grateful. You did more than I could have expected.

Test 1 Units 1–13

Choose the best alternative to complete each sentence.

1. Sam did me a really good . . . . when he lent me his Paris flat for a week.
a. change **b.** decision **c.** scene **d.** turn

2. What was absolutely . . . . was the view from the top of the mountain.
a. amazing **b.** amusing **c.** interesting **d.** shocking

3. Paul will bet on anything. He's a . . . . gambler.
a. compulsive **b.** hysterical **c.** impulsive **d.** terminal

4. I want the truth! I'm fed up with . . . . answers.
a. economical **b.** constructive **c.** evasive **d.** permissive

5. My . . . . is to proceed with the improvements despite the cost.
a. argument **b.** approval **c.** pronouncement **d.** recommendation

6. I'm pretty tired so if you don't mind, I'll . . . . for the night.
a. hold on **b.** work on **c.** work out **d.** turn in

7. Terry will never get married. He's a . . . . bachelor.
a. dissident **b.** confirmed **c.** radical **d.** strong

8. Bill and Sue both admit their marriage has been . . . . for years now.
a. on the rocks **b.** out of sorts **c.** at sea **d.** out of order

9. Unfortunately, your pen . . . . and left a bad stain on my shirt.
a. inflated **b.** flowed **c.** leaked **d.** squeezed

10. I'd put a . . . . around your suitcase for extra security.
a. strap **b.** lace **c.** plug **d.** string

11. This home-made wine of yours is extremely . . . . !
a. fatal **b.** lethal **c.** potent **d.** toxic

12. This dessert is delicious! I'd love a second . . . .
a. helping **b.** palate **c.** plate **d.** serving

13. We've tried . . . . persuasion, but Mike just will not apply for the job.
a. free **b.** total **c.** gentle **d.** strong

14. On Sundays there's free . . . . to all museums and galleries.
a. reduction **b.** prices **c.** entries **d.** admission

15. Why not have the fax . . . . for a week and see how you get on with it.
a. on credit **b.** on trial **c.** display **d.** on purpose

Test 2 Units 14–26

Choose the best alternative to complete each sentence.

1. Faulty goods can only be changed if you have a . . . .
   a. permission **b.** permit **c.** receipt **d.** recipe
2. It's been a good year. Profits greatly . . . . all expectations.
   a. adhered to **b.** affected **c.** exceeded **d.** remunerated
3. If you keep coming late, you . . . . the risk of losing your job.
   a. bear **b.** make **c.** suffer **d.** run
4. Ever since he caught that virus, Brian's been a bit . . . .
   a. off colour **b.** run out **c.** degenerate **d.** on the mend
5. Charlie was very . . . . about forgetting my birthday.
   a. awkward **b.** dedicated **c.** apologetic **d.** enthusiastic
6. I wonder if you could give me a . . . . to get these cases down.
   a. hand **b.** shoulder **c.** head **d.** arm
7. John's so serious. He really ought to let his . . . . down sometimes.
   a. eye **b.** hair **c.** hands **d.** mouth
8. There were about 8 of us . . . . into John's old car.
   a. bumped **b.** crammed **c.** cranked **d.** crunched
9. The hotel collapsed because its . . . . were too weak.
   a. basics **b.** bottoms **c.** foundations **d.** fundamentals
10. The doctor did what she could to . . . . the pain.
    a. agonise **b.** weaken **c.** cultivate **d.** alleviate
11. When we got to the phone box, it had been . . . .
    a. vandalised **b.** terminated **c.** terrorised **d.** mugged
12. And we've only got an hour left! This could be . . . .
    a. dreary **b.** drowsy **c.** spicy **d.** tricky
13. Dominic was really upset when his proposal was . . . .
    a. forbidden **b.** refused **c.** rejected **d.** retreated
14. As night came we decided to . . . . the search.
    a. abandon **b.** loosen **c.** withdraw **d.** deteriorate
15. What have you been getting . . . . recently? – Oh, nothing much.
    a. through to **b.** out of **c.** over **d.** up to

Test 3 Units 27–39

Choose the best alternative to complete each sentence.

1. Mark pinned his name badge onto his . . . .
a. lace **b.** lapel **c.** collar **d.** cuff

2. What a carry on! The . . . . tyre also had a puncture!
a. extra **b.** additional **c.** spare **d.** supplementary

3. After the accident, traffic was . . . . down some side streets.
a. diverted **b.** averted **c.** swerved **d.** dodged

4. I wasn't convinced of the product – even after the very . . . . presentation.
a. deadly **b.** headstrong **c.** slack **d.** slick

5. The famous star's love life was never out of the gossip . . . .
a. columns **b.** headlines **c.** tabloids **d.** headlines

6. The . . . . of the film said it was very disappointing.
a. caption **b.** review **c.** editorial **d.** article

7. The party was meant to be a surprise, but Keith let the . . . . out of the bag.
a. dog **b.** pig **c.** rat **d.** cat

8. I smell a . . . . I think it is all one big con trick!
a. bull **b.** rat **c.** pig **d.** snake

9. Tina sprained her . . . . when she fell.
a. leg **b.** wrist **c.** foot **d.** hand

10. There's been an . . . . increase in productivity recently.
a. appreciable **b.** appreciative **c.** intolerant **d.** intolerable

11. The quality of Sharon's work leaves a lot to be . . . .
a. decided **b.** consider **c.** desired **d.** pondered

12. A great deal of . . . . was levelled at the producer of the play.
a. objection **b.** comment **c.** consequence **d.** criticism

13. We can't do any more now. Let's call it a . . . .
a. day **b.** halt **c.** stop **d.** night

14. I'm . . . . tempted to tell him exactly what I think of him.
a. fully **b.** openly **c.** perfectly **d.** sorely

15. It's . . . . impossible to tell the two products apart.
a. flatly **b.** highly **c.** reluctantly **d.** virtually

Test 4 Units 40–52

Choose the best alternative to complete each sentence.

1. Have you decided yet? – Yes, we'll . . . . the cheaper option.
a. do up **b.** go for **c.** sort out **d.** take over

2. Sales were down so they had to . . . . some of their staff.
a. put out **b.** get out **c.** lay off **d.** turn down

3. We've carried out a . . . . survey of local transport facilities.
a. compatible **b.** comprehending **c.** comprehensible **d.** comprehensive

4. Why are you wasting your time going to yet another . . . . meeting?
a. unprofitable **b.** insurmountable **c.** irreplaceable **d.** unprintable

5. I'd like to welcome you all here . . . . Jimco Industries.
a. on account of **b.** on behalf of **c.** with a view to **d.** due to

6. Any increase in . . . . should be matched by a rise in salaries.
a. outcome **b.** outlook **c.** outline **d.** output

7. Are you in favour of . . . . punishment for premeditated murder?
a. clerical **b.** public **c.** capital **d.** national

8. You need total . . . . to become a world-class athlete.
a. commitment **b.** judgement **c.** appointment **d.** requirement

9. The climatic changes have been brought about by the . . . . effect.
a. domestic **b.** special **c.** greenhouse **d.** wet

10. You've got to learn all these facts . . . . for the exam.
a. by heart **b.** in hand **c.** on hand **d.** to heart

11. The lion . . . . as if to show that he was King of the Jungle.
a. barked **b.** grunted **c.** hooted **d.** roared

12. The snake . . . . away under a bush when we approached.
a. hopped **b.** swooped **c.** slithered **d.** prowled

13. The building is protected by highly . . . . warning devices.
a. sophisticated **b.** flexible **c.** considerable **d.** superficial

14. Go on! Stick your . . . . out! Tell us who is going to win!
a. arm **b.** head **c.** nose **d.** neck

15. In Sue's case, travel certainly . . . . the mind.
a. fastens **b.** tightens **c.** broadens **d.** loosens

Test 5 Units 53–65

Choose the best alternative to complete each sentence.

1. We aren't in . . . . to give you an answer right now.
a. a place **b.** a position **c.** a corner **d.** an agreement

2. We don't envisage any change in policy in the . . . . future.
a. enviable **b.** portable **c.** foreseeable **d.** nearest

3. The gang members were each . . . . to ten years in prison.
a. accused **b.** convicted **c.** prosecuted **d.** sentenced

4. Adam's mother was . . . . of shoplifting.
a. accused **b.** alleged **c.** compelled **d.** dismissed

5. I love the hustle and . . . . of the crowded market.
a. actions **b.** hurry **c.** bustle **d.** rustle

6. I really don't know what we would have done without your . . . . advice.
a. invaluable **b.** inviolate **c.** valued **d.** worthy

7. We must . . . . that all precautions have been taken.
a. assure **b.** suggest **c.** support **d.** ensure

8. I hate snakes so I was . . . . when one came near me.
a. dejected **b.** relieved **c.** petrified **d.** rejected

9. The hunters were . . . . by the thrill of the chase.
a. cheerful **b.** exhilerated **c.** contented **d.** irate

10. I don't mind . . . . as long as it is constructive.
a. apology **b.** gossip **c.** talk **d.** criticism

11. How can you . . . . acting in such a heartless manner?
a. justify **b.** assist **c.** regard **d.** require

12. I was in the . . . . position of trying to calm everyone down.
a. confidential **b.** suspicious **c.** responsible **d.** unenviable

13. I can't get a job. I think I must be on some kind of . . . . list.
a. black **b.** blue **c.** red **d.** green

14. We're going to paint the town . . . . to celebrate our win.
a. blue **b.** purple **c.** gold **d.** red

15. Don't worry! You'll soon get the . . . . of that machine.
a. hand **b.** hang **c.** range **d.** lie

Answers

1 A. 1.I'll 2.grown 3.bird 4.plain **C.** 1.patience 2.lengthening 3.entertainment 4.musician **D.**1.do 2.make 3.do 4.make 5.do 6.make foreseeable future, golden opportunity, lame excuse, radical change, recent past

2 1.irritated 2.depressed 3.shocked 4.interested 5.pleased 6.upset 7.annoyed 8.surprised 9.amazed 10.disappointed 11.amused 12.fascinated 13.amazing 14.amusing 15.interesting 16.disappointing 17.annoying 18.shocking

3 Set 1 1.d 2.c 3.a 4.j 5.i 6.g 7.b 8.f 9.e 10.h Set 2 1.d 2.h 3.a 4.i 5.f 6.e 7.b 8.g 9.j 10.c

4 1.application 2.approval 3.arrangement 4.confirmation 5.denials 6.development 7.dismissal 8.employment 9.examination 10.explanation 11.government 12.identification 13.pronunciation 14.recommendation 15.refusal 16.retirement

5 6.e 4.a 2.f 1.j 7.b 10.i 5.d 3.c 9.g 8.h 1.turn in 2.call for 3.look after 4.take off 5.get at 6.done up 7.worked out 8.put forward 9.hold on 10.cut down

6 1.d 2.b 3.d 4.a 5.a 6.b 7.c 8.c 9.b 10.a 11.a 12.c 13.c 14.b 15.b 16.d 17.c 18.a

7 1.m 2.h 3.o 4.e 5.b 6.j 7.n 8.i 9.g 10.d 11.l 12.a 13.c 14.k 15.f

8 1.bare 2.court 3.fare 4.flower 5.grown 6.heal 7.higher 8.missed 9.won 10.pale 11.piece 12.pair 13.rode 14.sale 15.scent 16.suite 17.week 18.hole

9 1.throat 2.cake 3.hair 4.paint 5.milk 6.light,lamp 7.balloon 8.verb 9.river 10.pen 11.pulse 12.trigger 13.tyre 14.dog

10 1.ladder, rung 2.shoe, lace 3.man, beard 4.hairdryer, plug 5.wheel, spoke 6.sink, taps 7.flower, petal 8.glass, stem 9.suitcase, strap

11 1.d 2.a 3.a 4.d 5.a 6.b 7.b 8.c 9.c 10.d 11.b 12.c 13.d 14.b

12 Set 1 1.g 2.i 3.e 4.a 5.d 6.j 7.c 8.h 9.f 10.b Set 2 1.e 2.b 3.a 4.j 5.i 6.h 7.d 8.g 9.c 10.f

13 1.trial 2.a diet 3.fire 4.the way 5.purpose 6.display 7.holiday 8.approval 9.condition that 10.credit 11.foot 12.behalf of 13.strike 14.the contrary

14 1.spectators 2.effect 3.beside 4.briefly 5.by 6.continual 7.inspected 8.for 9.headline 10.imaginative 11.permit 12.rise 13.receipt 14.sew 15.scenery 16.shadow 17.stationery 18.wandered

15 A. 1.commence (start) 2.comprehend (understand) 3.respond (reply) 4. advise (tell) 5.purchase (buy) 6.require (need) 7.exceed (be more than) 8.cease (end) 9.seek (look for)

B. 1.decline (turn down) 2.adhere (stick) 3.encounter(ed) (meet) 4.remit (send) 5.terminate (end) 6.ascertain (find out) 7.remunerate (pay) 8.obtain (get) 9.augment (increase)

16 Dressmaking: buttons, needles, pattern, pins, tape measure, thimble, thread Gardening: flowerpots, fork, hoe, hose, rake, spade, trowel Photography: camera, film, filters, flash, lens, light meter, tripod Woodwork: chisel, hammer, nails, plane, saw, screws, vice

17 1.d 2.b 3.a 4.c 5.b 6.d 7.d 8.c 9.a 10.c 11.a 12.c 13.b 14.d 15.d 16.d 17.c 18.c

18 1.difference 2.amends 3.pass 4.fortune 5.attempt 6.offer 7.day 8.example 9.contact 10.fun 11.ends 12.statement 13.bed 14.point 15.way 16.sense

19 1.decorator, dedicated, speculator, tranquilliser 2.certificate, competitor, delivery, impossible 3.decorations, dedication, electronic, entertainment 4.approximately, competitively, deteriorate, refrigerator 5.electricity, international, opportunity, representative 6.accommodation, apologetic, enthusiastic, investigation

20 1.hand 2.teeth 3.blood 4.bone 5.head 6.breast 7.blood 8.teeth 9.back 10.ear 11.back 12.head 13.heart 14.mouth 15.hair 16.hand 17.eye 18.leg 19.foot 20.hair 21.face 22.hand 23.face 24. tooth

21 1.d 2.b 3.a 4.a 5.d 6.b 7.b 8.a 9.c 10.c 11.c 12.d 13.b 14.a 15.c

22 Set 1 1.b 2.g 3.h 4.c 5.a 6.e 7.f 8.j 9.d 10.i Set 2 1.i 2.b 3.g 4.j 5.f 6.c 7.e 8.d 9.h 10.a

23 1.i 2.f 3.j 4.d 5.e 6.g 7.c 8.b 9.h 10.a

24 1.reject 2.denied 3.retreated 4.refused 5.defended 6.demolish 7.simplify 8.abandon 9.withdraw 10.deteriorated 11.forbidden 12.rewarded 13.lowered 14.set 15.fall 16.loosen

25 Set 1 1.i 2.f 3.b 4.h 5.g 6.j 7.c 8.e 9.a 10.d Set 2 1.round 2.over 3.together 4.out 5.on 6.away 7.up 8.through

26 Set 1 1.b 2.i 3.d 4.e 5.f 6.g 7.h 8.a 9.c 10.j Set 2 1.d 2.j 3.g 4.a 5.b 6.i 7.h 8.f 9.e 10.c

27 1.casualty, clinic, ward, X-ray 2.collar, cuff, lapel, sleeve 3.cooker, food mixer, fridge, sink 4.heel, lace, sole, toe 5.box office, footlights, stage, stalls 6.leaf, root, trunk, twig

28 1.d 2.b 3.c 4.b 5.c 6.c 7.a 8.c 9.c 10.c 11.a 12.d 13.c 14.c 15.b 16.d 17.b 18.a

29 2.block 3.clock 4.click 5.slick 6.slack 7.shack 8.shark 9.sharp 10.share 11.stare 12.spare 13.space 14.spice 15.spike 16.spite 17.spine 18.shine 19.whine

30 1.headline 2.circulation 3.review 4.gossip column 5.caption 6.tabloid 7.feature 8.cartoon 9.horoscope 10.preview 11.obituary 12.supplement 13.crossword 14.comic strip 15.editorial

31 1.worm 2.bat 3.bee 4.bull 5.cat 6.pig 7.chicken 8.bird 9.rat 10.crow 11.chicken 12.horse 13.dog 14.cat 15.bull

32 1.iron 2.rake 3.plaster 4.safety pin 5.hair grip 6.rug 7.hook 8.cheque 9.pencil 10.drinking straw 11.fence 12.spider 13.butterfly 14.ghost 15.shower 16.onion 17.doll 18.mug 19.ankle 20.wrist

33 Set 1 1.moan 2.damage 3.lying 4.appreciable 5.conscious 6.affect 7.accept 8.assumption 9.process 10.worthless 11.action 12.overcome 13.inconsiderate 14.treating 15.respectfully 16.current 17.As far as 18.intolerable 19.principal 20.consequences Set 2 1.wonder 2.to consider 3.watching 4.invented 5.Whether 6.leaves 7.criticisms 8.at 9.which 10.gets 11.breaks 12.However

34 Set 1 1.g 2.j 3.d 4.i 5.f 6.b 7.e 8.a 9.c 10.h Set 2 1.c 2.j 3.e 4.i 5.f 6.d 7.g 8.h 9.b 10.a

35 1.b 2.b 3.c 4.a 5.d 6.d 7.b 8.c 9.b 10.d 11.a 12.d 13.b 14.c

36 1.activity 2.consciousness 3.curiosity 4.familiarity 5.necessity 6.originality 7.possibility 8.reliability 9.regularity 10.sadness 11.seriousness 12.sensitivity 13.similarity 14.smoothness 15.speciality 16.weakness

37 1.virtually 2.highly 3.flatly 4.incredibly 5.fully 6.openly 7.greatly 8.perfectly 9.unreservedly 10.longingly 11.reluctantly 12.entirely 13.unconditionally 14.sorely 15.passionately 16.distinctly

38 1.d (dynamite) 2.f (I've a headache) 3.g (robbing banks) 4.k (lorry driver) 5.i (law and order) 6.m (persevere) 7.j (Ann drew pictures) 8.a (anorak) 9.e (carry me) 10.n (a mosquito) 11.h (Antarctic) 12.c (I'm alone) 13.b (sea shore) 14.l (maximum)

39 1.paper clips 2.guillotine 3.pencil sharpener 4.scissors 5.staples 6.punch 7.date stamp 8.wastepaper bin 9.string 10.tray 11.ruler 12. scales 13.stamps 14.notepad 15.stapler 1.punch 2.wastepaper bin 3.ruler 4.notepad 5.scales 6.string 7.guillotine 8.tray

40 8.h 6.a 7.i 9.c 3.d 1.e 2.g 4.f 10.b 5.j 1.go for 2.laid off 3.stick to 4.drop in 5.sort .. out 6.do up 7.turn down 8.get on 9.looks like 10.take over

41 1.eleventh 2.second 3.nineteen 4.two 5.second 6.forty 7.second 8.sixth 9.second 10.Ninety-nine 11.first 12.one 13.second 14.first 15.one

42 coma, comic, common, command, complain, community, completely, compartment, complication, comprehensive, comprehensible, compassionate or commiserating, compensation, communicate, commentate, commotion, commence, company, compel, comma, comb

43 Set 1 unattainable goal, incompatible lifestyles, illegible handwriting, unpalatable suggestion, unreliable source, insurmountable difficulties Set 2 inaccessible place, inadmissible evidence, unbearable heat, unenviable reputation, unprintable story, irreversible decision Set 3 incurable disease, indefensible action, inhospitable climate, implausible explanation, unprofitable meeting, irreplaceable component

44 1.c 2.a 3.c 4.a 5.c 6.c 7.b 8.d 9.b 10.b 11.d 12.b 13.a 14.c 15.b 16.b 17.c 18.d

45 1.bathroom cabinet 2.train set 3.watch 4.electric toaster 5.bath mat 6.shower 7.tennis racket 8.camera 9.sewing machine 10.garden hose 11.video recorder 12.tent 13.iron 14.petrol can 15.bathroom scales 16.electric fan

46 Set 1 1.g 2.a 3.f 4.b 5.j 6.e 7.h 8.d 9.i 10.c Set 2 1.d 2.g 3.b 4.c 5.a 6.e 7.f 8.i 9.h 10.j

47 1.e 2.i 3.k 4.a 5.m 6.d 7.c 8.g 9.o 10.l 11.f 12.n 13.b 14.j 15.h

48 1.c 2.d 3.b 4.b 5.c 6.a 7.b 8.b 9.a 10.c 11.a 12.b 13.a 14.c 15.b 16.a 17.b 18.b

49 1.c 2.m 3.i 4.a 5.k 6.e 7.d 8.j 9.l 10.h 11.f 12.b 13.g 14.slithered 15.galloped 16.hopped 17.prowled 18.swooped

50 1.clear 2.easy 3.graceful 4.harmful 5.approximate 6.guilty 7.even 8.scarce 9.superficial 10.flexible 11.considerable 12.crude 13.delicate 14.dim 15.compulsory 16.reluctant

51 1.teeth 2.hand 3.face 4.foot 5.nose 6.hands 7.back 8.face 9.foot 10.hands 11.legs 12.tongue 13.neck 14.heart 15.head 16.hand 17.feet 18.fingers 19.nose 20.arms 21.nose 22.eyes 23.hands 24.head

52 Set 1 1.d 2.e 3.h 4.f 5.c 6.a 7.b 8.g 9.j 10.i Set 2 1.i 2.g 3.a 4.h 5.e 6.b 7.c 8.j 9.f 10.d

53 1.charge of 2.favour of 3.fact 4.tears 5.silence 6.demand 7.a hurry 8.motion 9.the lead 10.private 11.a whisper 12.agreement 13.comparison with 14.a position to 15.the end 16.general

54. 1.answer, comfort, favour, gossip, honour, picture, question, shower, treasure, visit 2.attempt, control, decay, defeat, display, mistake, parade, regard, regret, support 3.conduct, convict, increase, present, produce, rebel, record, subject, suspect, transport

55 Set 1 1.d 2.g 3.e 4.f 5.i 6.j 7.h 8.b 9.c 10.a Set 2 1.e 2.a 3.c 4.b 5.j 6.g 7.d 8.i 9.h 10.f

56 1.b 2.b 3.a 4.d 5.c 6.d 7.c 8.c 9.b 10.b 11.b 12.c 13.b 14.b 15.b 16.a 17.n 18.c

57 Set 1 1.long 2.averse 3.bustle 4.pay 5.sun 6.However 7.wary 8.bread and butter 9.sensible 10.course 11.action 12.Nevertheless 13.worthless 14.ensure Set 2 1.advice 2.invaluable 3.raise 4.depressed 5.remind 6.appreciative 7.actions 8.accept 9.mistakes 10.distinct 11.say 12.prevent 13.bear 14.intolerable 15.alternative

58 1.annoyed, cross,furious, grumpy, infuriated, irate 2.apprehensive, intimidated, petrified, scared, startled, terrified 3.cheerful, contented, delighted, exhilarated, overjoyed, relieved 4.dejected, depressed, despondent, gloomy, heartbroken, miserable

59 Set 1 1.disagreeable 2.preferably 3.extensive 4.impassable 5.recognition 6.financially 7.suspicious 8.prosperity 9.divisive 10.unexpected 11.unwisely 12.spotlessly Set 2 1.decision 2.irresponsible 3.requirements 4.constructive 5.assistance 6.lengthened

7.notify 8.confidential 9.departure 10.misbehaved 11.pointless 12.unenviable Set 3 1.priceless 2.misunderstood 3.argument 4.non-smoker 5.apologise(ize) 6.truthful 7.unpredictable 8.pleasure 9.worthless 10.justify 11.unreasonable 13.impression, attention, appearance

60 Set 1 1.enthusiastic 2.capable 3.sorry 4.fed up 5.keen 6.good 7.crazy 8.typical
Set 2 1.excited 2.mad 3.fond 4.scared 5.sick 6.guilty

61 9.g 5.h 2.c 5.f 3.i 1.d 6.b 4.j 8.a 7.e 1.fixed up 2.keep on 3.put off 4.go over 5.tried .. out 6.stand by 7.breaks down 8.sit back 9. & 10.ran after, get away

62 1.SAILING AND BOATING 2.AUDIO & TV 3.ANIMALS AND PETS 4.CAMPING 5.DO IT YOURSELF 6.COLLECTING 7.HOUSES FOR SALE 8.MUSIC 9.ARTS & CRAFTS 10.PHOTOGRAPHY 11.LAND 12.OFFICE EQUIPMENT

63 1.red 2.green 3.black 4.black 5.red 6.white 7.blue 8.black 9.blue 10.red 11.black 12.black 13.red 14.green 15.black 16.green 17.red 18.black

64 Set 1 1.h 2.e 3.f 4.a 5.g 6.b 7.c 8.d
Set 2 1.e 2.d 3.g 4.h 5.a 6.f 7.c 8.b
Set 3 1.j 2.g 3.i 4.a 5.l 6.e 7.d 8.k 9.c 10.h 11.f 12.b

65 Set 1 1.d 2.f 3.c 4.b 5.h 6.a 7.e 8.i 9.g
Set 2 1.c 2.d 3.a 4.b

Test 1 1.d 2.a 3.a 4.c 5.d 6.d 7.b 8.a 9.c 10.a 11.c 12.a 13.c 14.d 15.b

Test 2 1.c 2.c 3.d 4.a 5.c 6.a 7.b 8.b 9.c 10.d 11.a 12.d 13.c 14.a 15.d

Test 3 1.b 2.c 3.a 4.d 5.a 6.b 7.d 8.b 9.b 10.a 11.c 12.d 13.a 14.d 15.d

Test 4 1.b 2.c 3.d 4.a 5.b 6.d 7.c 8.a 9.c 10.a 11.d 12.c 13.a 14.d 15.c

Test 5 1.b 2.c 3.d 4.a 5.c 6.a 7.d 8.c 9.b 10.d 11.a 12.d 13.a 14.d 15.b